Writing the Garden

A LITERARY CONVERSATION
ACROSS TWO CENTURIES

"One Approach to the Garden from the Sun Room." Frontispiece,
My Wild Flower Garden: The Story of a New Departure in Floriculture
by Herbert Durand, 1927.

Writing the Garden

A LITERARY CONVERSATION
ACROSS TWO CENTURIES

Elizabeth Barlow Rogers

NEW YORK SOCIETY LIBRARY &
FOUNDATION FOR LANDSCAPE STUDIES
IN ASSOCIATION WITH
DAVID R. GODINE, PUBLISHER

This book published in 2011 by
DAVID R. GODINE · PUBLISHER
Post Office Box 450 · Jaffrey, New Hampshire 03452
www.godine.com

༺༄༅༅

This book accompanies the exhibition
*Writing the Garden: Books from the Collections of
The New York Society Library & Elizabeth Barlow Rogers*
organized in 2011 by The New York Society Library.
The exhibition and book are generously supported in part
by Deborah S. Pease.
The publication of *Writing the Garden: A Literary Conversation Across
Two Centuries* was made possible with funding from the Foundation
for Landscape Studies and The New York Society Library.

LIBRARY OF CONGRESS CATALOGING-IN-PUBLICATION DATA

Rogers, Elizabeth Barlow, 1936-
Writing the garden : a literary conversation across two centuries / Elizabeth
Barlow Rogers. -- 1st ed.
  p. cm.
This book accompanies the exhibition "Writing the Garden" organized in 2011 by
The New York Society Library.
ISBN 978-1-56792-440-4
1. Horticultural literature. 2. Gardening in literature. I. Foundation for
Landscape Studies. II. New York Society Library. III. Title.
SB318.3.R64 2011
808.8'0364--dc22

2011008238

First edition, 2011

PRINTED IN CHINA

Contents

꧁꧂

CONTENTS

Preface

꧁꧂

 I t gives us great pleasure to present *Writing the Garden: Books from the Collections of The New York Society Library & Elizabeth Barlow Rogers* to our members and the public at large. The exhibition, which opened on May 12, 2011, in the Peluso Family Exhibition Gallery, was co-curated by Harriet Shapiro, the New York Society Library's Head of Exhibitions, and Elizabeth Barlow Rogers, the author of the book you now hold in your hands.

A few words about the history of the New York Society Library are in order here. Founded in 1754 by six prominent New Yorkers—William Smith Jr., William Livingston, John Morin Scott, Philip Livingston, Robert R. Livingston, Sr., and William Alexander—it is the city's oldest library. Its first home was in the "Library Room" at City Hall; then as the residential city moved uptown from the tip of Manhattan, it relocated in 1856 to 67 University Place and, finally, in 1937 to its current building designed by Trowbridge and Livingston at 53 East 79th Street. Over time the library's collection has grown from approximately 2,000 books to more than 300,000. Among these are numerous volumes on subjects related to gardens and gardening, a number of which are recognized as literary gems.

Elizabeth Barlow Rogers's career as a park preservationist, author, and collector of rare books on landscape history, garden design, and horticulture should also be outlined in brief. As many New Yorkers know, Rogers is a principal founder of the Central Park Conservancy, the public-private partnership responsible for transforming Central Park from a state of severe disrepair to its present status as New York City's crown jewel. She subsequently founded the Foundation for Landscape Studies and currently serves as its president. Her books include *The Forests and Wetlands of New York City* (1971), *Frederick Law Olmsted's New York* (1972), *Rebuilding Central Park: A Management and Restoration Plan* (1987), *Landscape Design: A Cultural and Architectural History* (2001), and *Romantic Gardens: Nature, Art, and Landscape Design* (2010). In addition, she is the editor of the journal *Site/Lines*, a publication of the Foundation for Landscape Studies.

I am grateful to Elizabeth Barlow Rogers for her essential role in this project. In addition, I appreciate the support of the boards of the New York Society Library and the Foundation for Landscape Studies, the sponsors of the publication of this book in association with David R. Godine, Publisher. Finally, the library thanks Deborah S. Pease for her support of the exhibition and book.

Mark Bartlett
HEAD LIBRARIAN
THE NEW YORK SOCIETY LIBRARY

Foreword

༄༅༅

*From putting together the experiences of gardeners in
different places, a conception of plants begins to form.
Gardening, reading about gardening, and writing
about gardening are all one; no one can garden alone.*

—Elizabeth Lawrence, *The Little Bulbs*, 1957

THE GENESIS of this book was an invitation from Mark
Bartlett, Head Librarian of the New York Society Library, to
co-curate with Harriet Shapiro, Head of Exhibitions, a display
featuring the library's trove of rare books by garden writers
along with similar works from my own collection. An afternoon
of delightful browsing with Harriet brought us to the same con-
clusion—that we should focus on a particular genre of garden
writing within the larger realm of books on landscape subjects:
books *by* and *for* actual gardeners. Moreover, these should be
books whose literary quality ensured even a nongardener's
reading pleasure.

It was difficult to leave on the shelf one of the library's great
treasures, the 1728 English edition of Dézallier d'Argenville's
The Theory and Practice of Gardening, but this treatise codifying
the design style of Louis XIV's royal gardener André Le Nôtre
falls outside our selective purview. Mentioning it here, however, provides a clue to the riches of the New York Society Library. It is remarkable that books such as the Dézallier, which

command high prices by rare book dealers when available today, are not recent acquisitions by the library, but rather were purchased not long after their original publication dates. Their status as rare books, therefore, is often a function of the long span of time they have been in the catalogue of more than three hundred thousand volumes that this venerable subscription library has amassed since its founding in 1754.

My own association with the New York Society Library began two centuries later, in 1964, the year I took up residence in the city. The Children's Library was an obvious boon to me as the mother of a young child, but an even greater asset was revealed around four years later when I began to research my first book, *The Forests and Wetlands of New York City* (1971). I remember going into the stacks and finding *Springs and Wells of Manhattan and the Bronx, New York City, at the End of the Nineteenth Century* (1938) by James Reuel Smith, as well as other similarly obscure titles. Although, as a member of the library, I could have borrowed these books, it was pleasanter to sit at a writing table in the high-ceilinged, second-floor reading room making research notes on a yellow legal pad in the midst of engrossed book lovers on nearby sofas and chairs.

Probably because I am a native of San Antonio, the first rare book I purchased for myself was Frederick Law Olmsted's *A Journey through Texas; or A Saddle-trip on the Southwestern Frontier* (1857). I felt bold that day in the late sixties when I stood at the counter of the Strand Bookstore writing a check for fifty dollars. Of course, I could have found this volume along with all of Olmsted's other books in the New York Society Library, but establishing a tangible link with America's first landscape architect was a catalytic event, prompting first the writing of *Frederick Law Olmsted's New York* (Whitney Museum/ Praeger, 1972) and then twenty years' involvement in the restoration of Central Park.

Buying this bit of Olmstediana also planted a seed that remained dormant until the 1990s. By then I was embarked on tracing landscape history both backwards and forwards from Olmsted, gathering material and visiting parks and gardens in other countries in preparation for writing *Landscape Design: A Cultural and Architectural History* (Abrams, 2001). Doing research in the rare-book rooms of libraries with collections that elucidate the history of landscape design with period images—Avery, Morgan, New York Public, Dumbarton Oaks, Harry Ransom Center, Hunt Institute, and Huntington, to name the most prominent—was an eye-opening experience. How fascinating those beautifully illustrated books by Humphry Repton were with their hand-colored flaps hiding and revealing before and after views! And what a thrill to hold an album containing prints of Versailles by Israel Silvestre or Nicolas and Adam Perelle! And turning the pages of the marvelous folios of engravings by Giovanni Battista Falda and Giovanni Francesco Venturini depicting the villas in and around Rome was almost as exciting as a trip to Italy.

Obtaining my own copy of Dézallier, which discusses and illustrates the French classical design idiom of Le Nôtre, was exciting enough to awaken the acquisitive streak that leads to the self-gratifying malady called collector's passion. Like most collections, mine has a particular focus: it principally consists of treatises on landscape theory and practice, books of engravings of historic landscapes and narratives, such as Olmsted's *Journey*, in which landscape description is a major theme. Some of these works are discussed in *Romantic Gardens: Nature, Art, and Landscape Design* (The Morgan Library & Museum in association with David R. Godine, Publisher, and the Foundation for Landscape Studies, 2010), and a number of them were on loan to the 2010 exhibition of the same title at the Morgan Library and Museum, for which I served as co-curator.

The books of mine discussed here in conjunction with ones belonging to the New York Society Library are a distinct subset within my overall collection. They were not acquired with any notion of collectability in mind but rather because I had succumbed to another passion: gardening. I can date the beginning of this phase of my life to a trip to England in 1974. It was to be the first of many subsequent trips to look at gardens and parks. My itinerary took me into Kent and Sussex Counties south of London, to the Cotswolds and the West Country, and then back east through Oxford. En route I visited Gravetye Manor, Nymans, and Sheffield Park in Sussex; Sissinghurst in Kent; Stourhead near Salisbury; Hidcote Manor and Sezincote in the Cotsworlds; Westbury Court and Kiftsgate Court in Gloucestershire; Knightshayes Court in Devon; Stowe in Buckinghamshire; and Blenheim Palace in Oxfordshire. I loved them all—the great eighteenth-century estate gardens of Stourhead and Blenheim, the Victorian splendor of Knightshayes, William Robinson's counter-Victorian landscape at Gravetye, and probably most of all Major Lawrence Johnston's Hidcote. It was in this garden that I experienced the epiphany that gardening is an art form like painting or architecture and that it was possible, with enough looking and learning, for a novice like me to make a garden myself.

Before that revelatory trip I grew marigolds, zinnias, lettuce, and tomatoes in the back-yard of my weekend home in Wainscott on the South Fork of Long Island. Now I was overcome with a desire to grow old heritage roses with names like 'Maiden's Blush' (or more erotically in French, 'Cuisses de nymphe,' or "nymph's thighs"). Catalogues from nurseries such as White Flower Farm in Connecticut, Wayside Gardens in Ohio (now in South Carolina), and Roses of Yesterday and Today in California began to arrive in the mail. I ordered bulbs from Holland—anemones, grape hyacinths, fritillarias, and scillas along with narcissuses, daffodils, and tulips. And I bought books not only about how to garden but books that friendly experts appeared to have written just for me, the amateur gardener. As I began to write this book and to select with Harriet the contents of the New York Society Library's corresponding exhibition, I discovered that these old books I had acquired willy-nilly over the years fit exactly the genre we had chosen as our thematic focus.

The sharing across time and distance of gardening news, tips, information, observations, and opinions found here is paralleled by the collaborative nature of this book. As Elizabeth Lawrence, one of my favorite garden writers, observes in the

epigraph above, "No one can garden alone." Certainly no author can produce a book such as this one without the skills of a
good editor and talented designer, the commitment of a sympathetic publisher, and the generosity of financial supporters.

In my case, I must first acknowledge Julia Moore, an editor of art history books with whom I have had a long professional and personal friendship. I am most appreciative of
Julia's attention to this essay's overall structure and narrative flow as well as her sound suggestions wherever she encountered infelicities of phrasing, a task that was augmented
by copy-editor Margaret Oppenheimer. Harriet Shapiro
provided a good editorial sounding board. I am grateful for
her discovery of certain volumes in the New York Society
Library that I might not have found on my own, as well as
her first-reader's suggestions regarding improvements to the
text. Brandi Tambasco of the Library also contributed her
valuable editorial skills. In addition, I am indebted to Judith
B. Tankard, landscape historian and author of *Gardens of the
Arts and Crafts Movement* (2004), *Beatrix Ferrand: Private Gardens, Public Landscapes* (2009), and *Gertrude Jekyll and the Country House Garden* (2011), for her helpful editorial comments and
manuscript corrections.

A further debt of gratitude is owed David Godine, a paragon within a dying breed, the independent book publisher. A
true bibliophile schooled in the craft of letterpress printing,
David involves himself in all aspects of his books' production. In this case we were immensely advantaged by having
Jerry Kelly as the book's designer. Jerry is a calligrapher as

well as a teacher of graphic design, and his skill is apparent in the layout, typeface, paper quality, cover, and other creative decisions that account for the book's handsome appearance.

The sponsors of the publication of *Writing the Garden* are the New York Society Library and the Foundation for Landscape Studies. Their underwriting of editorial, photographic, design, and other necessary expenses constitute a subvention without which it would have been prohibitive to publish the book in its present form. I am therefore grateful to Michael and Evelyn Jefcoat, longtime supporters of the Foundation for Landscape Studies, Frederic Rich, chairman, and the other board members for voting to underwrite a portion of these publication costs.

I offer thanks as well to Charles Berry, chairman, and the members of the board of the New York Society Library and to Mark Bartlett, head librarian, for encouraging me to bring together this array of garden writers from past generations along with those of our own time. Inevitably there are some fine garden writers missing from these pages. I hope that readers will discover them too, and that meeting the ones they will find here engaged in a timeless dialogue will make them want to read their books in their entirety.

Elizabeth Barlow Rogers
NEW YORK CITY

Introduction

I N THE SAME WAY that you don't have to be
a baseball fan to enjoy a good description of a
Yankees-Red Sox game by a sportswriter like
Roger Angell or to be a chef to savor the spice
in the books of a food writer like M. F. K. Fisher, you don't
have to be a gardener to appreciate the knowledge, enthusiasm, and wit with which certain garden writers achieve a
creative and fruitful liaison between words and nature. The
garden writers I have in mind are not the professional landscape designers whose theories, ideas, and examples provide
inspiration to garden-makers or the horticulturists and botanists whose works form the practical gardener's basic reference tools. Rather, they are the ones whose own gardens are
usually in full view as they write.

This does not mean that there is not a great deal of important information and sound instruction being conveyed
in this genre of garden writing—only that it is being deliv-
ered in informal, engaging, and sometimes droll literary prose.
Typically, authors in this category write in the first person.
This conversational style presumes a certain comradeship
with the reader. Some come across as friendly tutors. Others

create personae that make their words sound like neighborly nattering, gardener to gardener. Then there is the shriller voice of the polemicist with decided views on the proper approach to making gardens. In addition, there are the ruminations of the philosopher who finds the garden filled with metaphorical meaning.

I would say that all of the books of this genre are premised on passion. They constitute a love affair between the gardener and the garden. Although horticultural love affairs are often tumultuous (nature can be frustratingly fickle, and in dealing with weather, pests, and other adversities, some garden writers assume a comically beleaguered persona), the authors of these books are lovers of place, the space in nature the writer-gardener claims as home ground, an arena for individual creative expression. Naturally, the volumes we are about to discuss display varieties of tone, style, and intent. What unites them is their status as classics—books about gardens and gardening that we can read and reread simply for pleasure.

One could question the fact that, with the exception of Rousseau and Karel Čapek, a Czech, we are dealing here with anglophone writers. I believe that is so because the origin of this particular genre of garden literature is essentially a British innovation. Beginning with Alexander Pope's *Epistle to Lord Burlington*, which exhorts the garden-maker to "consult the Genius of the Place in all," the primacy of the English garden as a particular style of landscape design was established. Its alliance with the rural countryside laid the foundation for the Picturesque, and with the rise of Romanticism as an international movement, the *jardín anglais* became a kind of national export. Further, it is reasonable to suggest that a preponderance of garden writing was British because of the simple fact that landscape gardening and literature are this island nation's two principal art forms. Therefore one finds the garden serving as a setting in many English novels and providing the theme of many English poems.

As American gardening came of age in the nineteenth century, it was obviously to England that gardeners and landscape designers looked for advice, drawing on the works of J. C. Loudon and his wife Jane, proponents of the Gardenesque style, with its emphasis on horticultural display. Both Loudon and Andrew Jackson Downing, his American counterpart, edited gardening magazines as a means of communicating new botanical knowledge, garden-design theory, and horticultural information. As Gertrude Jekyll and other English garden-makers brought the genre of literature we are examining here to full flower at the turn of the twentieth century, it was natural that their American cousins would follow suit.

Differences in climate, history, and national ethos, however, account for divergent expressions between the two countries both in gardens and words. In Victorian England, sustained by a profession of trained head gardeners and their staffs, the Gardenesque style of specimen display enjoyed a longer period of fashion than in America. The subsequent Arts and Crafts movement helped foster a garden style that I like to think of as "Englishness Cherished." It is one where the mellow stone walls of ancient manor houses are married with seemingly casual floral compositions in which many of the plants once found in humble cottage gardens blend with rarer horticultural specimens. This is a place-specific kind of garden making. Estate-defined, it often enjoys a Picturesque alliance with the surrounding rural landscape, yet its fundamental design principle is one of enclosure. In America, however, as might be expected in a land of continental dimensions in which notions of wilderness and scenic grandeur have traditionally challenged the national imagination, the designers of the nineteenth-century villas in the Hudson River Valley and the turn-of-the-twentieth-century Country Place Era houses in the Berkshires were able to incorporate into their garden landscapes views of the more awesome scenery associated with the Romantic Sublime.

The present volume is, as the title suggests, a "literary conversation" for which I have provided the descriptive context for the voices of writers whose words appear along with mine. Garden writing flourishes today as vigorously as ever, and with so many wonderful books of this kind still being published, I do not feel that there should be an arbitrary cut-off date. Rather, I wish to set up a virtual colloquium that brings together garden writers from the end of the eighteenth century to the present.

Since even within a particular genre authors write from different perspectives and for diverse audiences, I have placed the garden writers we are about to meet within categories. There are those who write articles for magazines or columns for newspapers, which are sometimes collected and published in book form. These authors, along with the inveterate letter writers who thrive on horticultural fellowship with one another—often one and the same since garden columnists invariably receive mail from their readers—I call correspondents.

Other authors adopt the role of tutor, giving advice based on their own gardening experience and visits to other gardens. I have labeled them teachers. We also have here those whose random enthusiasms or strong opinions sound like the congenial musing or lively harangue you might hear over drinks. I have classified these writers as conversationalists.

Irony is a great literary virtue, and the gardener's foibles in the face of indifferent nature are the stuff of comedy. We therefore have a category of humorists. Then there are writers for whom the garden provides metaphors for subjects beyond botany, horticulture, and landscape design. I think of them as philosophers.

We meet women who broke the barrier of the spade; spouses who cooperated or quarreled; nurserymen who blurred the boundary between disinterested advice and business promotion; foragers who tell of their adventures digging plants for their gardens in the wild; warriors who filled their pens with vitriol in order to acidly disagree with one another; rhapsodists who never met a flower they didn't love tenderly; and travelers who write about the gardens of foreign lands. But, of course, teachers travel, travelers teach, philosophers can be humorous, humorists can philosophize, and so on. Therefore the reader should feel free to transpose these authors from one category to another as they see fit.

Transecting all our garden-writer categories are certain universal themes. Several of our authors tell us how their love of gardening sprang from a seed planted in childhood. The gardening mother or grandfather and the advantages of growing up surrounded by nature and horticulture were for them formative. These autobiographical fragments help round out our sense of their backgrounds, characters, and personalities, as well as their predilection for certain kinds of gardens.

Another theme that you will find sounded throughout is the importance of good soil. True gardeners always start in the most literal sense from the ground up. In their case "digging in the dirt" is much more than a metaphor. Soil is the fundamental medium of their art, and their close attention to its quality is a leitmotif that runs throughout our present survey. For them nothing is sweeter than the smell of freshly turned soil. More than any herbal fragrance, this is the most intoxicating garden aroma of all. Rightly, they give fundamental importance to knowing the degree to which their soil is composed of clay, sand, and silt and what its chemical composition is. To garden successfully, you, like they, must calculate your horticultural possibilities in terms of which plants will thrive in what kinds of soil. Read carefully what they have to say about soil when you are still a gardening neophyte; you will be grateful that they felt compelled to pass on this valuable information.

As a corollary requirement, competent gardeners need to

understand the climate of the region in which they garden and have a keen grasp of those plants that will thrive and those that cannot be planted at all. Related to this is a knowledge of the seasonal nature of gardening and which plants can be expected to appear to best advantage at various stages of the growing season. For this reason, you will note that many of the books under discussion have chapters titled according to the months of the year.

The Garden of Eden may have been the only garden not to have had aphids, scale insects, moth larvae, mealybugs, spider mites, cabbage worms, and a host of other unwelcome guests—including the slug, a slimy, shell-less mollusk. This nocturnal predator can ravage foliage and kill plants faster than they can grow. The slug is a universal scourge, the bane of gardeners everywhere, and a subject discussed with unqualified repugnance and unbridled ire by several authors we encounter in these pages.

Sensory delight, on the other hand, emerges as a happier recurring theme. There is a physicality to gardening, and we should take note of the tactile satisfaction dedicated gardeners find in good, friable soil running through their fingers; their joy in the pungent aroma of rich compost or decaying autumn leaves on a woodland path; the bliss they derive from the smell of various flowers in bloom; the aesthetic enjoyment they receive from tree form, plant texture, and flower structure, as well as the colors of bark, leaf, and blossom; the nostalgia they experience in remembering the taste of honeysuckle nectar when they were children.

Curiosity is a long suit among the garden writers we are considering. They are readers and researchers avid for botanical lore, horticultural history, and the etymology of plant names. They are steeped in the works of ancient and Elizabethan herbalists—Dioscorides, Pliny, Gerard—as well as Linnaeus and other pioneering botanists and plant hunters in the Age of Enlightenment. Because of the fact that self-taught amateur gardeners like to seek and share information and ideas and are quite naturally readers of one another, a large literary commonwealth of garden writers has developed during the past two and a half centuries. This is a situation that is hospitable to a personal and individualistic form of writing that presumes, as we shall soon see, a certain friendly intimacy between author and reader.

Women in the Garden

~

OR MORE than a century presumptions regarding the gardener's sexual identity have slowly undergone a sea change as perceptions about women gardeners have shifted from the commonly held belief of their being too delicate for dirt to the qualified notion of gardening as a suitable female occupation to their full admission as members of a now gender-irrelevant profession. Jumping the garden fence of Victorian values was a hurdle forward-thinking persons once had to encourage them to attempt. Later, a love of flowers and knowledge of plant form, color, and seasonal growth patterns opened the garden gate to a growing body of women who saw gardening as an art form. Gaining the same horticultural training and design skills as men, women at last were considered experts in the garden, putting them on an equal footing with their male peers. Throughout this long journey, ink from the pens of women garden writers never ceased to flow.

Jane Loudon

I would categorize Jane Loudon (1807–1858) as a pioneer on behalf of women gardeners as well as a botanical and horticultural educator of the first rank. Mrs. Loudon (she is thus referred to on the title pages of her books) was the wife of the Scottish botanist John Claudius Loudon (1783–1843), author of *An Encyclopedia of Gardening; Comprising the Theory and Practice of Horticulture, Floriculture, Arboriculture, and Landscape-Gardening* (1822). J. C. Loudon furthered the nineteenth-century marriage of industrial technology and horticulture with the invention of the hinged sash bar that made possible the construction of conservatories and glasshouses for the protection and propagation of the tender exotic plants pouring into England from the four corners of the world. He is best known as the originator of what is called the Gardenesque style, based on the arrangement of plants in a manner intended to display their characteristics as individual specimens.

A pioneer of science fiction like Mary Shelley, as Jane Webb (her maiden name), she anonymously published *The Mummy! Or a Tale of the Twenty-Second Century* (1827). Because of her descriptions of the kind of futuristic technological inventions that fascinated him, Loudon discovered the author's identity and arranged a meeting. After their marriage she served as her husband's amanuensis for the production of the rest of his herculean literary output, including the magisterial *Arboretum et Fruticetum Britannicum* (1838). Remarkably, she found time to become a botanical and horticultural writer herself. In *Instructions in Gardening for Ladies* (1840) and *The Ladies' Companion to the Flower Garden* (1841), she gently nudged her purportedly delicate female contemporaries to take up the spade and trowel and to dig and plant as a source of healthy exercise and self-fulfillment. Since the ladies to whom her words

"A Lady's gauntlet of strong leather, invented by Miss Perry of Stroud, near Hazlemere." *Gardening for Ladies; and Companion to the Ladies' Flower-Garden* by Mrs. Loudon, 1860.

are addressed were so unaccustomed to manual labor of this sort, she felt compelled to explain that "The first point to be attended to, in order to render the operation of digging less laborious, is to provide a suitable spade; that is, one which shall be as light as is consistent with strength, and which will penetrate the ground with the least possible trouble." In that era of normative female attire, it was necessary as well to suggest the appropriate costume for a lady gardener: "a pair of clogs . . . to put over her shoes; or if she should dislike these, and prefer strong shoes, she should be provided with what gardeners call a tramp . . . . She should also have a pair of stiff thick leathern gloves, or gauntlets, to protect her hands. . . ."

I particularly treasure my copy of Mrs. Loudon's *My Own Garden; or The Young Gardener's Year Book* (1855), a charming, small volume illustrated with exquisite hand-colored engravings depicting flowers of the four seasons. Her magnum opus, *The Ladies' Flower-Garden* (c. 1855–59), a five-volume botanical masterpiece, is much more than a book for women gardeners or children. Indeed, with its three hundred chromolithograph

"Tigridia pavonia. Common Tiger Flower." *The Ladies' Flower-Garden of Ornamental Bulbous Plants* by Mrs. Loudon, 1841.

"The splendid colours of this flower and the easiness of its culture render it a general favourite. Its only faults are, that its flowers have no fragrance, and that they are of very short duration. It is a native of Mexico, where it is called Ocoloxochitl. In its native country its bulb is considered medicinal; and it was on this account that it was sent to Europe by Hernandez, physician to Philip II of Spain, when he was employed by the Spanish government to examine into 'the virtues' of the plants of the New World. It has been also found in Peru. It was not introduced into England till 1796. The bulbs should be planted in the open ground in March or April, when they will flower in May or June, and they should be taken up in September or October, and tied in bunches, and hung in a dry place till spring. They are sufficiently hardy to be left in the ground in winter, were it not on account of the danger to which they are exposed from damp; and consequently if they can be kept quite dry they may remain in the ground. They will grow in any common garden soil, moderately rich, and not too stiff; but they succeed best where there is a mixture of sand, to allow of the free descent of the roots. When grown in pots, the soil should be sand and vegetable mould, or loam. The bulbs produce abundance of offsets; and the plants ripen plenty of seed, which it is worth sowing, as, contrary to the general habit of bulbs, the seedlings will frequently blossom the second year. Whenever the Tigridias are planted so as to form a bed, care should be taken to give them a back ground of grass or evergreens, on account of the great gorgeousness of their colours."

Pl. 8

1. *Tigridia pavonia* 2. *Tigridella flammea* 3. *Ferraria divaricata* 4. *Ferraria uncinata*

"*Papaver orientale*. Oriental Poppy." *The Ladies' Flower-Garden of Ornamental Perennials* by Mrs. Loudon, 1843.

"This is the handsomest of all the poppies. The flowers are very large, still more so than those of the preceding species, but in other respects at first sight they are scarcely to be distinguished asunder; though on closer inspection, it will be found that the hairs on the calyx and stem are closely pressed in a slanting direction, while those of the previous species spread horizontally. It also flowers a little earlier. It is a native of Mount Caucasus, and was introduced in 1817."

1. Papaver orientale _ 2. Papaver alpinum _ 3. Papaver rubro-aurantiacum _ 4. Meconopsis Cambrica _ 5. Argemone grandiflora _
_ 6. Sanguinaria Canadensis _ 7. Meclurgo violata.

plates and detailed descriptions of more than a thousand species in various categories—bulbs, annuals, perennials, greenhouse plants, wildflowers—it ranks as one of the most beautiful, useful, and readable botanical encyclopedias of all time.
The fact that Jane Loudon's Christian name was never used
in ascribing the authorship of this or her other books, and
that her principle role was that of her husband's amanuensis,
should not obscure the fact that his star pupil was his peer
in terms of horticultural and botanical knowledge and literary productivity. Accompanying every plate depicting related
individuals of a particular flower species are comprehensive accounts of each one's appearance, botanical structure, growth
habit, native origin, medicinal and other uses, and horticultural requirements. When I once saw a set of these sumptuous
volumes in the library at Garland Farm in Bar Harbor, Maine,
the final home of the pioneering landscape garden designer Beatrix Farrand, I realized that, unlike some other books containing exquisite botanical illustrations, *The Ladies' Flower-Garden*
could be a useful reference tool for professional as well as amateur gardeners, an observation that still holds true today.

Frances Garnet, Viscountess Wolseley

*H*alf a century later, as Victorian attitudes toward woman's place were beginning to relax, Frances Garnet, 2nd Viscountess Wolseley (1872–1936), could go one step further
than Jane Loudon in terms of encouraging women to become
gardeners. In 1902 she founded the College for Lady Gardeners in Glynde, Sussex, a school to educate female students to

do the same kind of horticultural labor—digging beds, preparing the soil, planting, weeding, watering, harvesting—that was the traditional domain of men. In opening the door of the previously all-male world of horticultural employment to women, she was well ahead of her time. (It was not until 1932 when Beatrix Havergal started the Waterperry School of Horticulture that a handful of women followed the founder in achieving recognition by the prestigious Royal Horticultural Society.)

When Wolseley wrote *In a College Garden* (1916), the world around her was rapidly changing. World War I had brought to a close the period when houseguests strolled along gravel paths set between wide planting beds bordered by clipped hedges and tea was carried by servants across verdant lawns to people lounging in wicker chairs in the shade of ancient trees. Sounding very much like the headmistress she had been before turning the operation of her college over to a former student who ran it according to the strict principles she had established, she reflected on her creation of "a garden complete enough to afford ample preparation to those women who wish to make a livelihood by gardening."

Like Mrs. Jane Loudon, Viscountess Wolseley felt it necessary to attire the female gardener "in the way of dress which is neat and yet essentially becoming and feminine." She believed that the student uniform should be simple, practical, and tidy, describing it thus:

> It consists of coat and skirt, khaki in colour, because the earth here, having so much lime in it, is light-coloured, and

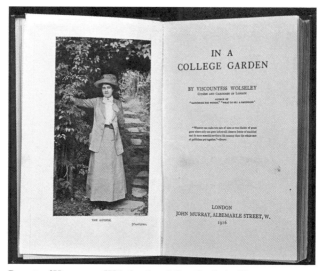

Portrait of Viscountess Wolseley. *In a College Garden* by Viscountess Wolseley, 1916.

therefore does not show upon drab-coloured cloth. Over this when busy [the students] wear a Hessian canvas apron containing roomy pockets for knife, raffia, tarred twine, and many other requisites that a gardener has constant need of. The skirts are what are called 'Aviation' ones, and are cut so that in windy weather, although they are short, they always cling neatly to the figure. Brown boots and leggings are below, and students are thus able to walk in and out of rows of cabbages or other vegetables and plants on a rainy day without having that heavy, wet, and tiring drag which is the drawback of an ordinary skirt. . . . A white shirt and brown felt soft-rimmed hat complete the uniform, so that only touches of colour come from the hat and silk sailor tie, and both these are red, white, and blue, which are the colours of the College.

In a College Garden can be considered a professional memoir, whereas Wolseley's *Gardens: Their Form and Design* (1919) is aimed at advising a new generation of small-property owners on the art of garden making. Covering all manner of subjects—entrances, formal flower beds, garden ornament, hedge-enclosed garden rooms, kitchen gardens, rock gardens, topiary, treillage—it is a clear expression of the Arts and Crafts style of garden design, a blending of architectural form, historical tradition, and sophisticated floriculture.

Gertrude Jekyll

*T*he doyenne and, to a large degree, the inventor of this type of garden, Gertrude Jekyll (1843–1932) thought of the garden as would a painter. For her, gardening was horticultural picture making. "Picture making" is the right term. Over and over in books such as *Wood and Garden* (1899), Jekyll paints verbal pictures as she takes us on a series of walks through her garden, Munstead Wood. Moving from one picture to the next through her gallery of garden scenes, she points out those of special interest during a particular month of the year, while at the same time attuning our senses to seasonal sounds and odors.

For Jekyll, nature is the gardener's best guide. There are also lessons to be learned from "the little cottage gardens that help make our English waysides the prettiest in the temperate world." With epigrammatic succinctness she sums up perhaps better than anyone the deep satisfaction to be had from the physical enterprise of gardening. For her the purpose of such activity was to give "happiness and repose of mind, firstly and above all considerations, and to give it through the presentation of the best kind of pictorial beauty of flower and foliage that can be combined or invented."

Fortunate is the gardener who has always lived in a garden, and lucky is the child who is given a plot to garden when still quite young. Jekyll's charming book *Children and Gardens* (1908) begins on an autobiographical note: "Well do I remember the time when I thought there were two kinds of people in the world—children and grown-ups, and that the world really belonged to the children. And I think it is because I have been more or less a gardener all my life that I still feel like a child in many ways, although from the number of years I have lived I ought to know that I am quite an old woman."

Drawing on her own experiences as a child, Jekyll segues from vivid recollections of her first gardening endeavors and her attraction to specific scenes of nature's beauty found on youthful rambles to this kind of careful instruction:

> I said I would tell you about plans. A plan is a map of a small space on a large scale—you will see what scale means presently. The plan shows what it represents as if you were looking at it from above. If you lie on a table on your stomach and look over the edge, and if exactly below your eyes there is a dinner-plate on the floor, you see the plate in *plan*.

Thus is the young gardener taught how to lay out a garden; in similar grandmotherly age-to-youth language, using her own diagrammatic sketches, she makes the rest of the ABCs of creating a garden and growing plants easy for a child to grasp.

For Jekyll, gardening is essentially an aesthetic enterprise. While she believed that acquiring knowledge of the qualities of various types of soil and mastering horticultural methods is an important part of the gardener's education, she stressed the importance of training oneself to have "a good flower-eye." Light plays an important role, as does seasonality, in

Dorothea and Dinah at Orchards. *Children and Gardens* by Gertrude Jekyll, 1908.

the making of Jekyll's garden pictures. And color and growing habit are all-important considerations. Here, for instance, is how she describes her half-acre plantation of azaleas: "The whites are planted at the lower and more shady end of the group; next come the yellows and pale pinks, and these are followed at a little distance by kinds whose flowers are of orange, copper, flame, and scarlet-crimson colourings; this strong-coloured group again softening off into the woodland by bushes of the common yellow *Azalea pontica*, and its variety with flowers of larger size and deeper colour."

It is thus not surprising to learn that Jekyll was a painter before poor eyesight caused her to exchange her palette of pigments for one of plants. In *Colour in the Flower Garden* (1908) she continues to paint garden pictures with the same kind of compositional forethought as an artist who first sketches the outlines of a new work on canvas. To explain her design method, Jekyll illustrates the book with diagrams for various beds and borders. The originator of color themes, she depicts plans for a gold garden, an orange garden, a gray garden, a blue garden, and a green garden. In addition, she inserts between some of the pages foldout plans for other gardens at Munstead Wood, including her long main border, the September border of early Michaelmas daisies, the June iris border, and her hidden garden. Studying these we perceive how, in order to

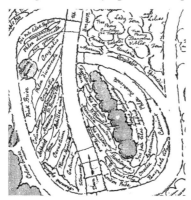

"Plan for the Hidden Garden" by Gertrude Jekyll. *Colour in the Flower Garden*, 1908.

achieve a tapestrylike weave of tone and texture, her flower schemes appear as loosely sketched, overlapping diagonal drifts. This approach to gardening is, of course, the antithesis of that of the Victorian gardeners who created precisely edged beds displaying showy annuals in patterned arrangements.

Above all, it is movement through the garden, the alternation of scenes from sunny lawn to shady woodland, that makes Munstead Wood such a delightful sensory experience. Here is how we begin our walk in her woodland garden:

My house, a big cottage, stands facing a little to the east of south, just below the wood. The windows of the sitting-room and its outer door, which stands open in all fine summer weather, look up a straight wide grassy way, the vista being ended by a fine old Scotch Fir with a background of dark wood. This old Fir and one other, and a number in and near the southern hedge, are all that remain of the older wood which was Scotch Fir.

This green wood walk, being the widest and most important, is treated more boldly than the others—with groups of Rhododendrons in the region rather near the house, and for the rest only a biggish patch of the two North American Brambles, the white-flowered *Rubus nutkanus*, and the rosy *R. odoratus*. In spring the western region of tall Spanish Chestnuts, which begins just beyond the Rhododendrons, is carpeted with Poets' Narcissus; the note of tender white blossom being taken up and repeated by the bloom-clouds of *Amelanchier*, that charming little woodland flowering tree whose use in such ways is so much neglected. Close to the ground in the distance the light comes with brilliant effect through the young leaves of a wide-spread carpet of Lily of

the Valley, whose clusters of sweet little white bells will be
a delight a month hence.

The Rhododendrons are carefully grouped for colour—
pink, white, rose and red of the best qualities are in the
sunniest part, while, kept well apart from them, near the
tall chestnuts and rejoicing in their partial shade, are the
purple colourings, of as pure and cool a purple as may be
found among carefully selected *ponticum* seedlings and the
few named kinds that associate well with them. . . .

Jekyll goes on to tell us how among the rhododendrons she
has planted strong groups of *Lilium auratum* to "give a new
picture of flower-beauty in the late summer and autumn." She
says that she has taken pains to make the garden melt imper-
ceptibly into the wood. Once you have entered it, a series of
paths diverging from the main grassy way call for different
combinations of shade-loving trees, shrubs, and ground covers. As she invites us to accompany her on the fern walk, she
wants us to understand that this is no wildwood but rather
one that is simply a naturalistic part of the garden proper:

> Just as wild gardening should never look like garden gar-
> dening, or, as it so sadly often does, like garden plants gone
> astray and quite out of place, so wood paths should never
> look like garden paths. There must be no hard edges, no
> conscious boundaries. The wood path is merely an easy way
> that the eye just perceives and the foot follows. It dies away
> imperceptibly on either side into the floor of the wood and
> is of exactly the same nature, only that it is smooth and easy
> and is not encumbered by projecting tree-roots, Bracken or
> Bramble, these being all removed when the path is made.

Penetrating deeper into the wood we find ourselves among oaks and birches.

> Looking round, the view is here and there stopped by prosperous-looking Hollies, but for the most part one can see a fair way into the wood. In April the wood floor is plentifully furnished with Daffodils. Here, in the region farthest removed from the white Poet's Daffodil of the upper ground, they are all of trumpet kinds, and the greater number of strong yellow colour. For the Daffodils range through the wood in a regular sequence of kinds that is not only the prettiest way to have them, but that I have often found, in the case of people who did not know their Daffodils well, served to make the whole story of their general kinds and relationships clear and plain; the hybrids of each group standing between the parent kinds; these again leading through other hybrids to further defined species, ending with the pure trumpets. As the sorts are intergrouped at their edges, so that at least two removes are in view at one time, the lesson in the general relationship of kins is easily learnt.
>
> They are planted, not in patches but in long drifts, a way that not only shows the plant in good number to better advantage, but that is singularly happy in its effect in the woodland landscape. This is specially noticeable towards the close of day, when the sunlight, yellowing as it nears the horizon, lights up the long stretches of yellow bloom with an increase of colour strength, while the wide-stretching shadow lengths throw the woodland shades into large phrases of broadened mass, all subdued and harmonized by the same yellow light that illuminates the long level rank of golden bloom.

This attention to the effects of light should alert us to the fact that Jekyll was an excellent photographer, and she can be credited with almost all of the illustrations in her books. Through the camera's lens as well as verbally, she captures her garden pictures in every season. Were we to take a tour of her woodland garden again in June after the spring bulbs have bloomed, we would see how the same yellowing light of late afternoon makes her careful color scheme of the rhodo-dendrons still more successful "by throwing its warm tone over the whole." But we should not forget to look down, for "nearer at hand the Fern walk has its own little pictures":

> In early summer there are patches of *Trillium*, the White Wood Lily, in cool hollows among the ferns, and, some twenty paces further up, another wider group of the same. Between the two, spreading through a mossy bank, in and out among the ferns and right down to the path, next to a patch of Oak Fern, is a charming little white flower. Its rambling roots thread their way under the mossy carpet, and every few inches throw up a neat little stem and leaves crowned with a starry flower of tenderest white. It is *Trientalis*, a native of our most northern hill-woods, the daintiest of all woodland flowers.

Carrying our eyes up from the ground are "the stately Foxgloves." Jekyll remarks, "It is good to see their strong spikes of solid bloom standing six to seven feet high, and then to look down again at the lowly *Trientalis* and to note how the tender little blossom, poised on its thread-like stem, holds its own in interest and importance." A bit farther along the fern walk near another group of *Trillium* is a patch of *Asa-rum virginicum*, a low-growing North American plant with shiny, roundish leaves and a wax-like brown and greenish flower, near which a little terrestrial orchid, *Goodyera repens*, is nestling in a tuft of moss. The fern walk ends where several other woodland paths intersect.

If we so wished, we could continue our delightful and instructive garden journey with Jekyll, but by now the reader will have perceived why her representation of the gardener as artist set so many subsequent English and American gardeners on the path toward making their own garden pictures. It is hard to think of the woman whom Edwin Lutyens called "Aunt Bumps" as being a revolutionary figure in landscape history. When, however, we meet other garden writers in this essay, we will see how many times she is referred to by them and the degree to which they are indebted to her for "a good flower-eye."

Sketch of Gertrude Jekyll digging a sunflower
by Edwin Lutyens, 6 August, 1897.

Warriors in the Garden
ᬢᬤᬢᬤ

GARDENING is nothing less than warfare with nature. With no respect for the cabbage or the rose, nature sends in her legions of hungry insects and foraging animals to wreak havoc. But there is another kind of warfare in the garden, one that is waged against fellow gardeners rather than garden pests. In this kind of warfare garden theory is often presented as a polemical diatribe against previous practices or contrary philosophies. For the reader, it is both instructive and amusing to argue or agree with certain opinionated writers and to refight the horticultural battles of yesteryear as they promulgate their passionate beliefs and ideas.

William Robinson

If Jekyll was the authoritative mother of a more naturalistic English garden style, her friend William Robinson (1838–1935) was its highly influential father. He also serves as the prime exemplar of a didactic and sometimes colorfully caustic genre of garden writing. In Robinson's view, the architect was the enemy of good landscape design, which he held to be the exclusive province of the gardener—that is,

the enlightened gardener who agreed with him that mowing be forsaken in some parts of the garden so that cut lawns
would transform themselves into wildflower meadows.
His further ideal was to allow climbing plants to entwine
themselves on trunks and branches, and he dogmatically
declared that fallen leaves should be left on the ground as
natural mulch in woodlands.

A trained professional gardener, Robinson had a botanist's
as well as a horticulturist's thorough knowledge of plant species and their growth habits. He was adamantly opposed
to greenhouse-grown annuals planted in regimental rows
or showy ornamental beds. He also detested the display of
trees and shrubs in Loudon's Gardenesque style as individual
specimens, and he vigorously proselytized the overthrow of
late Victorian gardening in favor of one in which bulbs were
planted in drifts, herbaceous beds were composed of mixed
perennials, and horticultural species appeared to merge at
the garden's perimeter with the native vegetation of meadows and woodlands. Together he and Jekyll redirected garden design in a way that gave the world what is now thought
of as the prototypical English garden—a blending of wild
and artificial nature; the grouping of trees and shrubs to form
pleasing landscape vistas; the use of hedges to create more
intimately scaled garden "rooms"; and the laying out of beds
in which casually composed yet sophisticated plant combinations—based on a thorough knowledge of floral and leaf
colors, blooming times, and growth characteristics—made
gardens interesting throughout the entire year.

Two years after the publication of *The English Flower Garden* (1883)—a volume that eventually ran to fifteen editions and remained in print for fifty years—Robinson purchased the Elizabethan manor of Gravetye in Sussex along with its adjoining two hundred acres. He subsequently acquired additional land so that his property totaled a thousand acres, more than sufficient in size for rural nature and naturalistic garden to be melded into a unified landscape with unobstructed views of the horizon. Here, with occasional advice from his friend Jekyll, he created broad scenic effects as well as herbaceous gardens closer to the manor. The landscape theories he put into practice at Gravetye, however, had been articulated long before in *The Wild Garden* (1870).

"Siberian columbine in a rocky place," engraving by Alfred Parsons from *The Wild Garden*, William Robinson, 1895 edition.

30

It would be a mistake, as Robinson is at pains to point out, to assume that the wild garden is the same thing as the native-plant garden. It should, to the contrary, be considered an opportunity to naturalize the flora of other countries, for as he tells us:

> Naturally our woods and wilds have no little loveliness in spring; we have here and there the Lily of the Valley and the Snowdrop, and everywhere the Primrose and Cowslip; the Bluebell and the Foxglove take possession of whole woods; but, with all our treasures in this way, we have no attractions in or near our gardens compared with what it is within our power to create. There are many countries, with winters colder than our own, that have a rich flora; and by choosing the hardiest exotics and planting them without the garden, we may form garden pictures.

Here it is important to pause a moment and consider again the term "garden pictures," since it is so frequently found in the writing of both Robinson and Gertrude Jekyll. For these writers, garden pictures did not imply the same thing as the Picturesque, the term commonly used to describe the earlier garden style in which designed landscapes were created in accordance with the principles of landscape painting. The garden pictures they had in mind are perhaps better characterized as vignettes, small scenes of beauty that the eye takes in as discrete discoveries rather than as panoramic scenery. Jekyll's carefully positioned camera framed many charming, seasonal vignettes within Munstead Wood, and in *The Wild Garden*, Alfred Parsons's engravings give graphic expression to Robinson's words, which are never themselves lacking in descriptive power. This does not mean, however, that such garden pictures, whether verbal or illustrational, should be considered as so many floral incidents independent of the overall landscape composition. Rather, the term is intended to imply that gardening is fundamentally an art form in which composition, color, line, and texture are as important as botanical knowledege and horticultural expertise.

Marshaling his arguments in favor of wild gardening, Robinson points out:

> Hundreds of the finest flowers will thrive much better in rough places than ever they did in the old-fashioned border; . . . look infinitely better than they ever did in formal beds; . . . [have] no disagreeable effects resulting from decay; . . . enable us to grow many plants that have never yet obtained a place in our 'trim gardens'; [and] settle the question of the spring flower garden [since] we may cease the dreadful practice of tearing up the flower-beds and leaving them like new-dug graves twice a year. As a final point in its favor, the wild garden can be seen as a kind of paradisiacal reunion of nature's bounty, for from almost every interesting region the traveler may bring seeds or plants, and establish near his home living souvenirs of the various countries he has visited.

Robinson's luxuriously produced *Gravetye Manor, or Twenty Years' Work Round an Old Manor House* (1911), is both a diary and a narrative of the successive stages of Gravetye's creation from 1885 through 1908. He tells the reader how he went about felling trees to open up views, removing iron trellises and the kitchen garden abutting the house, eliminating "a mass of rock-work (so-called) of ghastly order," and destroying other offensive elements left by the previous owners. The book's beautiful engravings evince the principles put forth in *The Wild Garden* as Robinson demonstrates Gravetye to be the paradigm in which house, garden, fields, and forest are united in a pastoral work of art as quintessentially English as a painting by Constable.

As attractive as all this may sound, there were some who felt that Robinson's garden ideal lacked cohesive structure. His peppery personality made it inevitable that he would be attacked by those who disagreed with him, most notably the architect Reginald Blomfield, whose ideas about what a garden should be were quite different.

Reginald Blomfield

The Formal Garden in England (1892) by the country-house architect Reginald Blomfield (1856–1942), with its attractive engravings by F. Inigo Thomas, is a treatise in the form of an essay on English garden history. In the preface to my second-edition copy Blomfield puts forth a spirited defense against what he considers to be Robinson's fallacious, intemperate, and untenable charges, made after the publication of the first edition. With considerable invective Robinson had taken issue with Blomfield's recommendations for a return to formality, and here it is Blomfield's turn to aim a few angry verbal arrows at Robinson. Heatedly, he rebuts Robinson's sarcastic barbs, accusing him of willful misinterpretation and ignorance of garden making as a form of art:

Mr. Robinson neither gives us the definition, nor shows us where the art is or what it consists of. The trees are beautiful, and so are the flowers, but where is Mr. Robinson's art? What does it do for us, or for the trees or the flowers? His skill as a tree-planter, or as a flower-grower, is no doubt great, but that does not make him an artist, and by no possible wrestling of the term can he be called so on this ground only.

Blomfield maintained, "The formal treatment of gardens ought, perhaps, to be called the architectural treatment of gardens, for it consists in the extension of the principles of design which govern the house to the grounds which surround it." Discriminating between the two views of gardening—the formal and the naturalistic—he argues:

> The formal school insists upon design; the house and the grounds should be designed together and in relation to each other; no attempt should be made to conceal the design of the garden, there being no reason for doing so, but the bounding lines, whether it is the garden wall or the lines of paths and parterres, should be shown frankly and unreservedly, and the garden treated specifically as an enclosed space to be laid out exactly as the designer pleases.

He strongly refutes the notion that the landscape gardener has a monopoly on nature:

> The clipped yew-tree is as much a part of nature—that is, subject to natural laws—as a forest oak; but the landscapist, by appealing to associations which surround the personification of nature, holds the clipped yew-tree to obloquy as something against nature. Again "nature" is said

to prefer a curved line to a straight, and it is thence inferred that all the lines in a garden, and especially paths, should be curved. Now as a matter of fact in nature—that is, in the visible phenomena of the earth's surface—there are no lines at all; "a line" is simply an abstraction which conveniently expresses the direction of a succession of objects which may be either straight or curved. "Nature" has nothing to do with either straight lines or curved; it is simply begging the question to lay it down as an axiom that curved lines are more "natural" than straight.

For Blomfield, it was not the Italian style of formal gardening that was instructive for contemporary gardeners; rather it was the old gardens of England that had not succumbed to the fashion for Baroque ornamentation or, subsequently, the Picturesque. Nor did formality imply a great expanse as in the French garden, for "some of the best examples of [the English garden] are on a comparatively small scale." However, Blomfield does not merely sing the praises of old English formal gardens. With an architect's eye for composition and detail, he criticizes these as well as the later gardens designed in the Picturesque style, his principal objects of censure. He maintains that the white marble statues of Bacchus and Flora at Wilton were a mistake: "To attain its full effect [marble] wants strong sunlight, a clear dry light, and a cloudless sky. In the soft light and nebulous atmosphere of the north marble looks forlorn and out of place." An integrated overall plan is what counts most, so in discussing public parks he comes down hard on "the spasmodic futility" of Battersea Park where, without a dominant idea controlling the general scheme, "merely to introduce so many statues or plaster casts is to begin at the wrong end. These are the accidents of the system, not the system itself."

Blomfield is united with Robinson, however unintentionally, in despising the Gardenesque style and the gardener who would have the specimen dahlia banish the hollyhock and other simple, old-fashioned flowers. He equally hates plants in beds that "make the lawn hideous with patches of brilliant red varied by streaks of purple blue." Taking sarcastic aim at the Victorian head gardener, he asks, "Would he plant them in patterns of stars and lozenges and tadpoles? Would he border them with paths of asphalt? Would he not rather fill his borders with every kind of beautiful flower that he might delight in, and set them off with grass and pleasant green?"

In Blomfield's mind, the desired relationship between the architect and the horticulturist should not end in a stand-off, nor would it, if their responsibilities were divided thusly: "The designer, whether professional or amateur, should lay down the main lines and deal with the garden as a whole, but the execution, such as the best method of forming beds, laying turf, planting trees, and pruning hedges, should be left to the gardener, whose proper business it is."

In this regard, it is worth noting that Gertrude Jekyll achieved some of her most notable gardens in collaboration with the architect Edwin Lutyens. Their sympathetic marriage of brick terracing and hedge-enclosed garden spaces created an Arts and Crafts landscape idiom that influenced Vita Sackville-West and Harold Nicolson at Sissinghurst and many other gardeners up to the present day. Providing an architectural frame uniting house and garden and giving structure to seasonal borders of sophisticated horticultural artistry, this type of design might be viewed as a synthesis of Robinson and Blomfield. The harmonizing of their opposing but ultimately complementary theories resulted in a style that made a virtue of formal structure as a foil for loosely composed "garden pictures." In this way these important late-nineteenth-century garden writers can be said to have assisted in the redirection of English garden style at a critical time when vast estate grounds were beginning to become a thing of the past.

Watercolor by Childe Hassam. Frontispiece, *An Island Garden* by Celia Thaxter, 1895.

Rhapsodists in the Garden

❦

Paradise is a synonym for *garden*, and the garden is often a paradise in the minds of those whose happiest hours are spent in one. In the case of certain garden writers this is a state that gives rise to ecstatic description. Theirs is a passion we experience with vicarious enthusiasm, an infectious rapture that makes us believe that gardeners are perhaps the happiest of all mortals.

Celia Thaxter

Celia Thaxter (1835–1894) spent almost her entire life on the coast of Maine where her father, Thomas Laighton, was a lighthouse keeper. After her marriage at the age of fifteen, she and her husband, Levi Thaxter, ran Laighton's summer hotel, Appledore House, on one of the Isles of Shoals; and it was here that she created and cultivated with a never-flagging passion the garden she describes in *An Island Garden* (1895). Although Thaxter thought of herself primarily as a poet and was certainly a prolific one, her verse has not stood the test of time very well. This much-loved book, however, is an enduring classic.

Each spring, after spreading rich barnyard compost on top of the thin soil of Appledore's rocky bluffs, Thaxter planted a garden. Only fifteen by fifty feet in size with nine geometrical flower beds, its profusion of summer annuals, propagated from seed in her winter home on the mainland, gave it a riotous grandeur. This fecund display is matched by Thaxter's prose, which often verges on the euphoric.

Because of her childhood love affair with plants and nature, Thaxter found her gardener's destiny early in life. Her book, like Jekyll's *Wood and Garden*, recounts a formative story, when as a "lonely child living on a lighthouse island ten miles away from the mainland, every blade that sprang out of the ground, every humblest weed, was precious in my sight, and I began a little garden when not more than five years old." Thaxter was hardly a lonely woman, however, for Appledore Hotel, where she presided as hostess, served for many years as a popular New England artists' and writers' summer colony. The guests included such luminaries as Emerson, Hawthorne, Whittier, Longfellow, William Morris Hunt, and Childe Hassam, whose watercolor paintings of Thaxter's garden were reproduced as chromolithograph illustrations in *An Island Garden*.

Although her profuse garden offered an abundance of painterly scenes—it could perhaps be best characterized as an American Impressionist garden, as Hassam's illustrations amply testify—Thaxter does not speak about the art of garden design per se. Hers is a spiritual prose as she writes of her own passionate responses to the ways in which plants perform and of the extremes to which she will go in nurturing them. A poppy seed is "the merest atom of matter, hardly

visible a speck, a pin's point in bulk, but within it is impris-
oned a spirit of beauty ineffable, which will break its bonds
and emerge from the dark ground and blossom in a splendor
so dazzling as to baffle all powers of description. The Genie in
the Arabian tale is not half so astonishing." She then sums up
her possession of a green thumb in one word, LOVE. This is the
motive force that causes her to fill wooden boxes with well-
rotted manure into which she nestles the cut eggshells with
pricked bottoms that will serve as the containers in which her
precious poppy seeds will germinate, after which she will gently place the delicate roots of the seedlings in the ground.

Love, however, does not extend to Thaxter's garden
enemies—"the cutworm, the wire-worm, the pansy-worm,
the thrip, the rose-beetle, the aphis, the mildew, and many
more, but worst of all the loathsome slug, a slimy, shapeless
creature that devours every fair and exquisite thing in the
garden." To combat this despicable garden marauder, "the
flower lover must seek these with unflagging energy, and if
possible exterminate the whole." It takes considerable wili-
ness to wage war on these nocturnal raiders. Thaxter tells us
how at sunset she heaps air-slaked lime in rings around her
flower beds as a barrier to the slug. Night patrol is also needed to conquer this determined pest, and she confesses how on
"many a solemn midnight have I stolen from my bed to visit
my cherished treasures by the pale glimpse of the moon, that I
might be quite sure that the protecting rings were still strong
enough to save them." She also combats this obnoxious terrestrial mollusk with salt; however, afraid that salt, like lime,

"The Garden in its Glory." Watercolor
by Childe Hassam. *An Island Garden*
by Celia Thaxter, 1895.

may prove injurious to her tender plants, she removes both in the morning when the slug has gone back into hiding beneath the ground. As an extra precaution to make sure they escape injury, as the ocean air and dew might dissolve these toxic substances into the soil, she collars her most beloved "pets" with rings of cut pasteboard and places her lime and salt on these.

Thaxter suddenly becomes excited by advice from a friend on the mainland who, anticipating the advocates of biological pest control, tells her that toads like to dine on slugs. She immediately responds, "In the name of the Prophet, Toads!" and soon receives by mail boat a box with sixty of them. They grow fat and multiply, and the next summer she imports ninety more. But toads, too, have their enemies—dogs and rats—and so the ranks of these garden warriors diminish. Nevertheless Thaxter manages to keep a sufficient number at work in the garden destroying slugs and insects, and therefore feels compelled to suggest that "every gardener should treat [the toad] with utmost hospitality . . . and, should he wander away from [the premises] to go so far as to exercise gentle force in bringing him back to the regions where his services may be of the greatest utility."

Although Thaxter's garden was haphazardly planned in terms of color combinations, her focus on the individual flower shows a remarkable level of aesthetic discrimination. Examining a California poppy, she has this to say:

The stems and fine thread-like leaves are smooth and cool gray-green, as if to temper the fire of the blossoms, which are smooth also, unlike almost all other poppies, that are crumpled past endurance in their close green buds, and make one feel as if they could not wait to break out of the calyx and loosen their petals to the sun, to be soothed into even tranquility of beauty by the touches of the air. Every cool gray-green leaf is tipped with a tiny line of red, every flower-bud wears a little pale-green cap like an elf. Nothing could be more picturesque than this fairy cap, and nothing more charming than to watch the blossom push it off and spread its yellow petals, slowly rounding to the perfect cup. . . . It is held upright on a straight and polished stem, its petals curving upward and outward into the cup of light, pure gold with a lustrous satin sheen; a rich orange is painted on the gold, drawn in infinitely fine lines to a point in the centre of the edge of each petal, so that the effect is that of a diamond of flame in a cup of gold. It is not enough that the powdery anthers are orange bordered with gold; they are whirled about the very heart of the flower like a revolving Catherine-wheel of fire. In the centre of the anthers is a shining point of warm sea-green, a last consummate touch which makes the beauty of the blossom supreme.

It is not surprising to learn that Thaxter's garden was

mainly a cutting garden for the flowers she arranged with exquisite care, placing them in orchestrated ranges of hue and tint in her music room. One visitor to Appledore House remarked, "I have never seen such realized possibilities of color! The fine harmonic sense of the woman and artist and poet thrilled through these long chords of color, and filled the room with an atmosphere which made it seem like living in a rainbow."

"The Altar and the Shrine." Watercolor by Childe Hassam.
An Island Garden by Celia Thaxter, 1895.

Alice Morse Earle

Alice Morse Earle's (1851–1911) career as an American garden writer coincided with the rise of the Colonial Revival movement in the 1890s. For Earle, a social and cultural historian, the Colonial Revival, which had been sparked by the Centennial Exposition of 1876 in Philadelphia, was more than a period style to be copied; the period it recalled was one to be celebrated for its simple virtues and agreeable customs. It is true that, beyond being an appreciation of the mores of the country's early settlers, the Colonial Revival was a nativist response to the admission of approximately a million immigrants annually into the United States. Although Earle was not immune from the prejudices of other Wasps, her attitude toward immigrants was merely patronizing as opposed to xenophobic.

In such books as *Customs and Fashions in Old New England* (1893), *Colonial Dames and Goodwives* (1895), *Colonial Days in Old New York* (1896), *Costume of Colonial Times* (1894), *Home Life in Colonial Days* (1898), and *Child Life in Colonial Days* (1899), Earle conveyed with rosy pen the customs of the bygone period that was her subject. Besides being a celebration of colonial horticulture, *Old Time Gardens* (1901) contains much garden and plant lore. Its focus is broader than the beauty of colonial gardens, white-picket-fenced enclosures resembling an English cottage garden in size and appearance. Earle wrote about the fine gardens of her own day, including the Hunnewell topiary gardens overlooking Lake Waban in Wellesley, Massachusetts, and the gardens at Yaddo, the Sarasota Springs estate that Spencer Trask converted into an artists' retreat in 1900 as a gift to his wife, Katrina. Regarding the latter, Earle writes that the Yaddo Rose Garden "formed a happy surprise to the garden's mistress" when unveiled at its dedication. She praises its "quality of expression, of significance, [which] may be seen in many a smaller and simpler garden, even in a tiny cottage plot." She adds that "you can perceive, through the care bestowed upon it, and its responsive blossoming, a *something* which shows the life of the garden owners; you know that they are thoughtful, kindly, beauty-loving, home-loving."

My copy of *Old Time Gardens*, one of an edition of three hundred and fifty copies printed on special paper, contains a number of beautiful photogravures. Together they constitute a portfolio of American gardens at the turn of the twentieth century, before two world wars, changing economic conditions, altered career expectations for women, an emphasis on

"Garden at Mount Vernon-on-the-Potomac. Home of George Washington." *Old Time Gardens* by Alice Morse Earle, 1901.

sports recreation, and modernist functionalism diminished the loving care once lavished on them. The peaceful charm of the gardens depicted in these illustrations—with lush, box-bordered flower beds; sundials; balustraded terraces; and rose-covered pergolas—evokes that idyllic moment in the history of American landscape design when the Arts and Crafts and Colonial Revival movements, combined with the influence of Italian Renaissance villas, made many gardens in this country rival contemporary ones in England.

Like Thaxter, Earle had a literary bent, and *Old Time Gardens* is laced with many quotations and verses of poetry. Here, in words reminiscent of Thaxter's, she singles out the poppy for poetic praise:

> There is something very fine about a Poppy, in the extraordinary combination of boldness of color and great size with its slender delicacy of stem, the grace of the set of the beautiful buds, the fine turn of the flower as it opens, and the wonderful airiness of poise of so heavy a flower. The silkiness of tissue of the petals, and their semi-transparency in some colors, and the delicate fringes of some varieties, are great charms.
>
> *Each crumpled crêpe-like leaf is soft as silk;*
> *Long, long ago the children saw them there,*
> *Scarlet and rose, with fringes white as milk,*
> *And called them 'shawls for fairies' dainty wear';*
> *They were not finer, those laid safe away*
> *In that low attic, neath the brown, warm eaves.*
>
> And when the flowers have shed, oh, so lightly! their silken petals, there is still another beauty, a seed vessel of such classic shape that it wears a crown.

It is not surprising that Earle devotes an entire chapter to "Childhood in a Garden." She promoted her belief that "the intense enjoyment of nature is a sixth sense" with this explanation:

> We are not born with this good gift, nor do we often acquire it in later life; it comes through our rearing. The fullness of delight in a garden is the bequest of childhood spent in a garden. No study or possession of flowers in mature years can afford gratification equal to that conferred by childish associations with them; by the sudden recollection of flower lore, the memory of child friendships, the recalling of games or toys made of flowers; you cannot explain it; it seems a concentration, an extract of all the sunshine and beauty of those happy summers of our lives when the whole day and every day was spent among flowers. The sober have grown up knowing not when 'the summer comes with bee and flower.'

Recalling her own childhood in the garden in " 'little cubby houses' under the close-growing stems of Lilac and Syringa, with an old thick shawl outspread on the damp earth for a carpet," she says:

> Let us peer into these garden thickets at these happy little girls, fantastic in the garden dress. Their hair is hung thick with Dandelion curls, made from pale green opal-tinted stems that have grown long under shrubbery and Box borders. Around their necks are childish wampum, strings of Dandelion beads or Daisy chains. More delicate wreaths for the neck and hair were made from the blossoms of the Four-o'clock or the petals of Phlox or Lilacs, threaded with pretty alteration of color. Fuchsias were hung at the ears for eardrops, green leaves were pinned with leaf stems into little caps and bonnets and aprons, Foxgloves made dainty children's gloves. Truly the garden-bred child went in gay attire.

There were sensory as well as sartorial experiences to be savored. Earle confides, "I never walk through an old garden without wishing to nibble and browse the leaves and stems which I ate as a child, without sucking a drop of honey from certain flowers. I do it not with intent, but I waken to realization with the petal of Trumpet of Honeysuckle in my hand and its drop of ambrosia on my lips."

"The Children's Garden." *Old Time Gardens* by Alice Morse Earle, 1901.

Calling our attention to one illustration, she writes:

[This] is a glimpse of a Box-edged garden in Worcester, whose blossoming has been a delight to me every summer of my entire life. In my childhood this home was that of flower-loving neighbors who had an established and constant system of exchange with my mother and other neighbors of flowers, plants, seeds, slips, and bulbs. The garden was serene with an atmosphere of worthy old age; you wondered

"An Old Worcester Garden." *Old Time Gardens* by Alice Morse Earle, 1901.

how any man so old could so constantly plant, weed, prune, and hoe until you saw how he loved his flowers, and how his wife loved them. The Roses, Peonies, and Flower de Luce in this garden were sixty years old, and the Box also; the shrubs are almost trees. . . . Here bloom Crocuses, Snow-drops, Grape Hyacinths, and sometimes Tulips, before any neighbor has a blossom and scarce a leaf. On a Sunday noon in April there are always flower lovers hanging over the low fences, and gazing at the welcome early blooms. Here if ever,

> *'Winter, slumbering in the open air,*
> *Wears on his smiling face a dream of spring.'*

A close cloud of Box-scent hangs over this garden, even in midwinter; sometimes the Box edgings grow until no one can walk between; then drastic measures have to be taken, and the rows look ragged for a time.

Elizabeth von Arnim

*E*lizabeth von Arnim (1866–1941), an English novelist, became famous for her first book, *Elizabeth and Her German Garden* (1898), which was so immediately popular that it ran to twenty printings in the initial year of its publication. Couched in the form of a diary, it describes the free-spirited author's efforts to become a gardener in the face of the mores of aristocratic society in provincial Germany and the duties imposed on her as the mistress of her husband's large Pomeranian estate.

Elizabeth, a nom de plume devoid of a surname (her maiden name was Mary Annette Beauchamp), was forced to disguise her identity at the request of her domineering husband, Count Henning August von Arnim-Schlagenthin, whom she refers to throughout her book as the "Man of Wrath." Some readers today will object to her high-handed treatment of servants and censorious attitude toward most of her visitors. To her credit, "German Elizabeth," as she became known to readers, scolds herself for being disagreeable when in pursuit of escape from the strictures of the Man of Wrath and the household responsibilities and social demands that take her away from her beloved garden:

> The garden is the place I go to for refuge and shelter, not the house. In the house are duties and annoyances, servants to exhort and admonish, furniture, and meals; but out there blessings crowd around me at every step—it is there that I am sorry for the unkindness in me, for those selfish thoughts that are so much worse than they feel; it is there that all my

sins and silliness are forgiven, there that I feel protected and at home, and every flower and weed is a friend and every tree a lover. When I have been vexed I run out to them for comfort, and when I have been angry without just cause, it is there that I find absolution. Did ever a woman have so many friends?

In addition to skirting the Man of Wrath's disapproval of the solitary hours she spends in blissful retreat in the garden, sometimes surrounded by her little ones—"the April baby, the May baby, the June baby"—rather than inside overseeing the domestic staff and the workers who are restoring the large old nunnery that serves as their family castle, Elizabeth must overcome her horticultural ignorance and accomplish the creation of her German paradise in the face of the gardener's stubborn insistence on laying out single plant varieties in regimented rows. The novice gardener can identify with her cheerful account of failed and successful experiments with different plant varieties and women readers with her spirit of subversive independence. We can all enjoy her joie de vivre as she revels in the scenery of nature when taking friends in a sleigh for a winter picnic beside the Baltic:

> The Man of Wrath loathes picnics, and has no eye for nature and frozen seas, and is simply bored by a long drive through a forest that does not belong to him; a single turnip on his own place is more admirable in his eyes than the tallest, pinkest, straightest pine that ever reared its snow-crowned head against the setting sunlight. . . . He went once and only once to this particular place, and made us feel so small by his blasé behavior that I never invite him now. It is a

beautiful spot, endless forest stretching along the shore as far as the eye can reach; and after driving through it for miles you come suddenly at the end of an avenue of arching trees, upon the glistening oily sea, with the orange-colored sails of distant fishing-smacks shining in the sunlight. Whenever I have been there it has been windless weather, and the silence so profound that I could hear my pulses beating. The humming of insects and the sudden scream of a jay are the only sounds in summer, and in winter the stillness is the stillness of death.

Continuing her career as a writer following the success of *Elizabeth and Her German Garden*, Arnim wrote several other semiautobiographical books, including *The Solitary Summer* (1899), *April Baby's Book of Tunes* (1900), *The Benefactress* (1901), *The Princess Priscilla's Fortnight* (1905), *Fräulein Schmidt and Mr Anstruther* (1907), and *The Caravaners* (1909).

More writer than gardener, as it turned out, this aristocratic woman of the world went on to publish *The Pastor's Wife* (1914), *Christine* (1917), *Christopher and Columbus* (1919), *In the Mountains* (1920), *Vera* (1921), *The Enchanted April* (1922), *Love* (1925), *Introduction to Sally* (1926), *Expiation* (1929), *Father* (1931), *The Jasmine Farm* (1934), *All the Dogs of My Life* (1936) and *Mr Skeffington* (1940) before her death in Charleston, South Carolina, in 1941. Throughout her prolific literary career, her identity remained firmly associated with her hugely successful first book, and the title pages of all her subsequent ones are ascribed to "The author of *Elizabeth and Her German Garden*."

Louise Beebe Wilder

*E*lizabeth von Arnim's American contemporary Louise Beebe Wilder (1878–1938) brought the style of rapturously Romantic garden writing to an audience with different growing conditions from those of Germany or England. Unlike "German Elizabeth," Wilder was anything but a novice gardener. She wrote nine garden books in all and also served as the editor of the journal of the Federated Garden Clubs of New York. Her passionate enthusiasm, vast knowledge of plants, and the verve with which she describes their aesthetic and sensory characteristics as well as their growth habits and climatic suitability have kept most of her books in print over the years. These include *My Garden* (1916), *Colour in My Garden* (1918), *Adventures in My Garden and Rock Garden* (1926), *Pleasures & Problems of a Rock Garden* (1928), *The Fragrant Path: A Book About Sweet Scented Flowers and Leaves* (1932), and *Adventures with Hardy Bulbs* (1936).

Wilder was extremely widely read and could summon as authorities many authors whose works touched on botany, horticulture, or the garden. She frequently consulted the herbalists John Gerard, who wrote the *Great Herball, or Generall Historie of Plantes* (1597), and John Evelyn, the author of *Kalendarium Hortense* (1664). Pliny, Shakespeare, Bacon, Montaigne, Horace Walpole, and even the prophet Muhammad could be counted on to embellish her words, and she constantly calls on Gertrude Jekyll as well as numerous other members of the intergenerational coterie of fellow garden writers to reinforce her opinions and advice.

My first edition of *Colour in My Garden* is a beautiful book with twenty-four color plates of Balderbrae—Wilder's garden in Pomona, New York—painted by Anna Winegar over the course of a single year. Looking at them, I sense within the more formal design structure of Balderbrae the same kind of casual luxuriance that Hassam captured in his paintings of Celia Thaxter's garden. Wilder's vivid descriptions of the garden and its plants, however, make illustrations superfluous. To sample her evocative prose, you can read what she has to say about poppies:

> The crepe-petalled Iceland poppy (*Papaver nudicaule*) that sows itself in my garden, springing up in the most unlikely nooks and crevices, has much of the airy charm of the annual sorts and decks itself in the loveliest colours: apricot and orange, buff, scarlet and white. I had from an English seedman this year a kind not too whimsically named Pearls of Dawn, for a rosy glow underlies the soft buffs and creams of its fragile petals.

She then contrasts its beauty with that of the Spanish poppy (*P. rupifragum*):

> It has all the whimsical appeal of its delicately bold race and hoists its little snatches of gay colour on stems as thin as wire. But there is nothing frail about the solid tuft of leaves or the mighty tap root that, when you essay to get it out of the ground intact, seems to reach to China. This plant, too, is as hardy as iron and unmindful of drought as it continues to send aloft its colour until frozen to inactivity.

Although she may sound as rhapsodic as Celia Thaxter or Alice Morse Earle when she is extolling the beauty of poppies, the similarity stops there. Wilder's garden was more than a colorful mélange of summer annuals jumbled together like

"Oriental Poppies and Valerian, May 28th." *Colour in My Garden* by Louise Beebe Wilder, 1927 edition.

Behind this brilliant group are strong clumps of *Gypsophila paniculata* which, by the time the Poppies are ready for a rather disorderly retreat underground and the yellowing stalks of the Valerian are cut down, has spread a rejuvenating web of wiry branches and delicate gray-green foliage above their heads and rescued the border from dire forlornity.

Thaxter's. Balderbrae was carefully planned according to the picturesque effects derived from various combinations of plant color and form. In addition, Wilder's considerable botanical expertise extended over a vast range of plants. As proof, *Colour in My Garden* contains sixty pages devoted to two appendices. The first contains the Latin and common names of thousands of plants in a list that goes from *Ambronia umbellate* (sand verbena) to *Zinnia* (youth-and-old-age). The second is a chart for periods of flowering, which Wilder has arranged according to plant color—a still useful aid to those interested in creating harmonious, seasonal garden pictures. Since the blooming dates are derived from the flowers in her own garden, she advises that "an allowance of a week should be made for each hundred miles north and south of the latitude of New York."

In *The Fragrant Path* Wilder makes the discerning nose the organ of garden pleasure. With the same botanical expertise as that displayed in *Colour in My Garden*, she follows each chapter with an annotated list of plants containing descriptions of their appearance, growth characteristics, and, often, the precise smells attributed to each. In addition, we learn this interesting fact: "For the most part fragrant flowers are light in colour or white. Brilliant flowers are seldom scented, though now and again there is an exception to prove the rule."

Along with such chapters as "Pleasures of the Nose," "The Sweets of May," "Summer and Autumn Scents," "Sweet Scented Flowers in the Rock Garden," and "Scents of Orchard and Berry Patch," Wilder includes one on "Plants of Evil Odour." With forthright candor it begins:

Stink is a robust old-fashioned word once in good social standing but having no character in polite society to-day. Our forefathers used it freely to characterize anything which appealed to them as of an unsavoury nature, whether a disagreeable experience, a damaged reputation, or a stench. That it was frequently applied to plants and with good reason we have only to open such books as 'A Dictionary of English Plant Names' to be assured. Therein we find a surprisingly long list of plants whose descriptive title in the vernacular was 'stink' or 'stinking,' and there are many whose unhappy secret is advertised by the Latin specific terminations *foetidus*, bad smelling; *graveolens*, heavy scented; *hircine*, goatlike odour, and the like.

She knew, probably from reading his famous *Diary*, that John Evelyn "did not like the smell of Box and referred more than once to the 'unagreeableness of its smell.' " She tells us as well that Thoreau thought that the carrion vine lived up to its name, since according to her, he claimed: " 'It smells exactly like a dead rat in the wall, and apparently attracts flies like carrion. . . . A single minute flower in an umbel, open, will scent a whole room.' " She advises us not to pick *Mentha arvenis*, the corn mint, "a gift of Europe to our spacious wild, [whose leaves] when bruised smell like stale cheese. If you gather it because of its pretty dark rose-coloured blossoms that appear in the late summer your regret will last until you reach home and can thoroughly wash your hands."

At the other end of the olfactory spectrum is, of course, the queen of flowers:

Fragrance is the rightful heritage of the Rose, and it is what we consciously or unconsciously expect of it. We cannot dissociate fragrance and the Rose. If you doubt this, watch the visitors at any Rose show bobbing forward automatically before each exhibit to inhale the fragrance and plainly registering by word or look pleasure or the reverse as the response they receive. . . . Of late, there has been uneasiness among flower lovers because of the numbers of scentless, or nearly scentless, Roses now appearing on the market. It is hard to believe that a scentless Rose could have great vogue, but there is that chill and soulless beauty, Frau Karl Druschki, to the contrary notwithstanding.

The curse of scentlessness is sometimes removed when the modern hybrid roses are crossed with old roses. Wilder's language then rivals that of the wine connoisseur when she describes certain hybrids of intricate and complex old-rose ancestry. In one instance she invites us to smell and detect "the odours of spice and musk and of honey, even that of Violets . . . and a whole gamut of fruity odours."

Like Jekyll, Earle, and other garden writers who grew up playing in a garden, Wilder's happy recollections of her youthful associations with nature and place reinforce one of the themes running throughout these pages: if there is such a thing as a horticultural gene, it is powerfully nurtured by the privilege of having been born into a gardening family and having lived in a home with a beautiful garden. In citing a repertoire of fragrant roses, Wilder says:

In the Maryland garden of my youth we grew only Teas and Noisettes and I remember that splendid Rose of the latter class, Maréchal Niel, that wound a vigorous wreath about the library windows, was called the Strawberry Rose, because its pointed golden buds so realistically suggested the pungent odour of ripe Strawberries, and that the Tea Rose, Safrano, my mother's favourite, had distinctly the spicy breath of the Scotch Pinks that edged the bed. . . . The Box bushes grew tall in my grandfather's garden in Massachusetts, which has been little changed in outline for more than a hundred years. Their sharp scent seemed to bring about a special atmosphere of apartness and mystery, and when mingled with the simpler scents of herbs and the old time Roses, after a shower or an early frost, the odours of this lovely old garden would be raised to such a pitch of oriental richness that one felt transported straight out of green and white New England to the glamorous East. And to a small person creeping through the white gate to play, the usual game of young matron tidily keeping house beneath the Grape vine and competently managing a large family of dolls, seemed no longer fitting. Instead a distraught lady out of the Arabian Nights glided with lissome grace up and down the straight paths, a fantastic head dress of Hollyhocks masking pigtails, a Lily scepter in her hand.

Thus are the imprinted memories of childhood the future gardener's lucky inheritance.

Nurserymen in the Garden

✦✦✦

ESIDES being businesspersons, some nurserymen have gone beyond their occupational re-
sponsibility of offering catalogue lists of their
botanical offerings and ventured into the realm
of garden writing. Particularly in the nineteenth century—
a time that saw an explosion of new plant varieties coming
into cultivation and the consequent development of a thriv-
ing nursery industry—a rising middle class, as yet unsure of
how to lay out and ornament the grounds of newly acquired
properties, formed a readership eager for instruction in the
design and planting of gardens. It is not surprising to find
the occasional nurseryman enlarging his traditional role and
joining the ranks of the Loudons and other authors of encyclopedic garden books as a purveyor of botanical information,
tasteful design advice, and practical horticultural knowledge.

Andrew Jackson Downing

The son of a nurseryman in Newburgh, New York, Andrew
Jackson Downing (1815–1852) acquired a thorough knowledge
of botany and the principles of landscape gardening before setting forth on a self-proclaimed mission to instruct new rural
property owners on how to build their homes and landscape

their villa grounds with taste—that genteel decorative sensibility that spelled social refinement.

In 1841, while still running the family nursery business, Downing published his first book, *A Treatise on the Theory and Practice of Landscape Gardening, Adapted to North America*. Its critical and commercial success as the first book of its kind in America gained him widespread recognition as a horticultural and landscape-design authority. *Cottage Residences* (1842), *Fruits and Fruit Trees of America* (1845), and *The Architecture of Country Houses* (1850) followed.

Beginning in 1846 Downing's magazine, *The Horticulturist*, gave him a literary platform from which to dispense horticultural information and promote his landscape-design theories. In a stream of regular articles he discussed the best methods of transplanting trees, enriching soil, fertilizing orchards, growing vegetables, producing wine, constructing ice houses and greenhouses, designing rural villas, and landscaping their grounds. In 1853, a year after his untimely death, Downing's best articles in *The Horticulturist* were collected in a single volume published as *Rural Essays* (1853). This book provides an important perspective on the degree of attention nineteenth-century Americans gave to landscape design as a core component of urban and regional planning, a sphere that encompassed the country's first suburbs, parks, parkways, and rural cemeteries, all of which were social responses to the rapidly industrializing new metropolis. The essays also provide revealing glimpses of mid-nineteenth-century American cultural mores and social attitudes.

In the essay titled "On Feminine Taste in Rural Affairs," Downing takes up the theme of women in the garden. *"What is the reason American ladies don't love to work in their gardens?"* he asks. The answer is:

> They may love to 'potter' a little. Three or four times in the spring they take a fancy to examine the color of the soil a few inches below the surface; they sow some China Asters, and plant a few Dahlias, and it is all over. Love flowers, with all their hearts, they certainly do. Few things are more enchanting to them than a fine garden; and *bouquets on their centre tables* are positive necessities, with every lady, from Maine to the Rio Grande.

By contrast:

> If anyone wants to know how completely and intensely English women enter into the spirit of gardening, he has only to watch the wife of the most humble artisan who settles in any of our cities. She not only has a pot of flowers—her back-yard is a perfect curiosity-shop of botanical rarities. She is never done with training, and watering, and caring for them. And truly, they reward her well; for who ever saw such large geraniums, such fresh daisies, such ruddy roses! Comparing them with the neglected and weak specimens in the garden of her neighbor, one might be tempted to believe that they had been magnetized by the charm of personal fondness of their mistress, into a life and beauty not common to other plants.

Downing rhetorically clinches his argument for turning American women into active gardeners: "EXERCISE, FRESH AIR, HEALTH,—are they not almost synonymous?" Nor will he brook argument from those who say, " 'But Mr.

Downing, think of the hot sun in this country, and our complexions!' " His reply:

> 'Yes, yes we know it. But get up an hour earlier, fair reader; put on your broadest sun-bonnet, and your stoutest pair of gloves, and try the problem of health, enjoyment and beauty, before the sun gets too ardent. A great deal may be done in this way; and after a while, if your heart is in the right place for ruralities, you will find the occupation so fascinating that you will gradually find yourself able to enjoy keenly what was at first only a very irksome sort of duty.'

Although Downing was the foremost advocate for a great metropolitan park in New York City and would most likely have been the designer of Central Park but for his untimely death in 1852, his most long-lasting influence was due to the definitive nature of *A Treatise on the Theory and Practice of Landscape Gardening*. This encyclopedic book had a twofold value: first, as a guide to place making and, second, as a practical manual on the names and uses of various plants. In it, he prophesied optimistically:

> The number of individuals among us who possess wealth and refinement sufficient to enable them to enjoy the pleasures of a country life, and who desire in their private residences so much of the beauties of landscape gardening and rural embellishment as may be had without any enormous expenditure of means, is every day increasing. And, although, until lately, a very meager plan of laying out the grounds of a residence, was all that we could lay claim to, yet the taste for elegant rural improvements is advancing now so rapidly, that we have no hesitation in predicting that in half a century more, there will exist a greater number of beautiful villas and country seats of

moderate extent, in the Atlantic States, than in any country in Europe, England alone excepted.

As testimony to its wide and enduring readership, Downing's *Treatise* was republished several times. My own sixth edition, which appeared in 1859, contains over a hundred steel and wood engravings. They provide an important record of Downing's influence on mid-nineteenth-century America's rising middle class, as farms were converted into rural residences called villas or cottages. It was according to the principles he expounded, and often with his on-site professional services, that owners elevated the appearance of their properties from unkempt barnyards to domains of refinement by "the removal or concealment of everything uncouth and discordant, and . . . the introduction and preservation of forms pleasing in their expression, their outlines, and their fitness for the abode of man."

Downing's *Treatise*, coupled with his background as a nurseryman, gained him widespread public recognition and reputation as a horticultural authority and tastemaker. Like Frederick Law Olmsted after him, he was influenced by English landscape theory and example. In forming his own approach to landscape design, he drew on the principles of both Humphry Repton and J. C. Loudon, remarking to his readers that "Repton's taste in Landscape gardening was cultivated and elegant," and "Mr. Loudon's writings and labors in tasteful gardening, are too well known to render it necessary that we should do more than allude to them here." American estates did not have to be as grand as the

"Example of the Beautiful in Landscape Gardening." *A Treatise on the Theory and Practice of Landscape Gardening* by Andrew Jackson Downing, 1859 edition.

countryseats in England in order to be landscaped in an elegant manner; they did, however, need to have the necessary compass to include broad vistas. As he explained, "Our art, to appear to best advantage, requires some extent of surface—its lines should lose themselves indefinitely, and unite agreeably and gradually with those of the surrounding country." The scenery throughout Downing's native Hudson River Valley, with its magnificent river views, was ideally suited to this Romantic ideal.

In the manner of the eighteenth-century aesthetic theorists in Britain, Downing sought in the *Treatise* to teach his readers how to discriminate between the Beautiful and the

"Example of the Picturesque in Landscape Gardening." *A Treatise on the Theory and Practice of Landscape Gardening* by Andrew Jackson Downing, 1859 edition.

Picturesque. He therefore had his engraver depict the Beautiful, or "graceful" as he alternatively calls it, as a female-inhabited environment with gently curving paths, softly rounded tree forms, and gracious Neoclassical architectural details, while directing him to portray the Picturesque with spire-like conifers, steeply pitched eaves, and other signs of spirited irregularity, ruggedness, and angularity that presumably accord with the masculinity of the huntsman and dog who complete the scene. The architecture compatible with the Beautiful was "Italian, Tuscan, or Venetian," whereas builders in the Picturesque style had as appropriate models "the Gothic mansion, the old English or the Swiss cottage" and were free to incorporate in their schemes various rustic features.

Downing's three underlying principles of good design, derived from Repton, were "UNITY, HARMONY, AND VARIETY"—*unity* being a controlling idea based on the nature of the site and "some grand or leading features to which the others should be merely subordinate"; *variety* the development of spectator interest through intricacy and ornamental details; and *harmony* the principle that ordered variety and made it subservient to the overall unity of the composition. Further, he tempered picturesqueness with practicality, declaring that "firm gravel walks near the house, and a general air of neatness in that quarter, are indispensable to the fitness of the scene in all modes." Concurring with Loudon, he maintained that "*recognition of art*" was "a first principle of Landscape Gardening . . . and those of its professors have erred, who supposed that the object of this art is merely to produce a facsimile of nature."

A large section of the *Treatise* comprises a descriptive catalogue of deciduous and evergreen ornamental trees. Here Downing does more than display his impressive store of botanical knowledge, dwelling upon aesthetic rather than scientific characteristics such as "the lights and shadows reflected and embosomed in [the oak's] foliage" and the "pleasing richness and intricacy in its huge ramification of branch and limb." He also points out the virtues of vines and other kinds of climbing plants with their "luxuriant and ever-varying forms." In the language of the Romantic, he says:

Climbing plants may be classed among the *adventitious beauties of trees*. Who has not often witnessed with delight in our native forests, the striking beauty of a noble tree, the old trunk and fantastic branches of which were enwreathed with the luxuriant and pliant shoots and rich foliage of some beautiful vine, clothing even its decayed limbs with verdure, and hanging down in gay festoon or loose negligent masses, waving to and fro in the air.

As in his chapter on trees, he provides a list of desirable climbing plants, including varieties of wisteria, woodbine, and honeysuckle, which will accomplish these effects.

An indispensable trove of horticultural information and gardening ideas in its day, the *Treatise* now serves as an important repository of architectural styles, landscape fashions, and planting practices of mid-nineteenth-century America. Together with *Rural Essays*, it portrays an aspiring nation ambitious to acquire the trappings of culture and refinement. In a country still insecure in its self-perception when comparing itself with the Old World, gardening with taste was, as Downing taught, an important sign of civilized society.

William Paul

I recently encountered someone less renowned than Downing when I found on my bookshelf a small, undated volume titled *The Hand-Book of Villa Gardening*, Third Edition (first edition, 1855), by William Paul (1822–1905). It turned out to be the work of a nineteenth-century British nurseryman who hoped to help amateur gardeners acquire sufficient horticultural sense and landscape sensibility to enable them to ornament their premises with taste. Paul, like Downing, ad-dressed himself to the prosperous, rising middle class whose properties, though not as vast as the great estates of the aris-tocracy, were sufficiently extensive to require design and or-namentation of the grounds. Like the Loudons, he advocated a Gardenesque plan, one aimed less at the creation of pictur-esque scenery than at accommodating botanical variety and interest. His ideal garden was one with a gently undulating lawn "dotted here and there with a *single evergreen* of rarity and beauty, and a *few vases*, clumps, or rustic baskets." There is an implicit assumption that his readers' financial resources allow them to afford greenhouses, conservatories, and other horticultural amenities, as well as an array of ornamental trees, fruit trees, shrubs, flowers, and vegetables, all of which presumably require a considerable amount of labor. However, his advice is seemingly directed to gardeners who—with the aid of such recently invented devices as the lawn mower—consider gardening a pleasant occupation. Toward this end, he employs the literary conceit of couching his chapters as replies to a friend who had supposedly written him letters requesting advice.

With Victorian virtue, Paul begins his first "letter" by ex-tolling the advantages of gardening as a source of recreation, believing "that an active mind requires something more than family and business matters to complete the sum of secular oc-cupation; and a 'hobby,' *rightly pursued*, rather than interfering with the great duties of life, intensifies the powers, and leads to a greater and more complete success." He furthermore advocates gardening as a family activity, one that should be entered into by women and children as well as men. In his letter on "The Children's Garden," he queries: "What quality of head and heart which gives grace and wisdom to the after life of English manhood and English womanhood is not nurtured and developed by the cultivation of flowers?"

With regard to layout at a time when eclecticism had replaced unitary landscape theory, it is not surprising for this nurseryman to recommend a visit to "the most celebrated nurseries and gardens in your neighbourhood, and, if possible those in different styles." In terms of garden features, in addition to vases and statues "appropriate in character, good in quality, and few in number," Paul suggests that "a temple or an arbour may be placed to advantage." To provide additional shade he recommends "an arcade, formed with rustic poles, and covered with roses, honeysuckles, and various

"Lawn Mower." *The Hand-Book of Villa Gardening* by William Paul, 1855.

summer-blooming climbers of rapid growth." As an important adjunct to the garden, there must be a compost yard, for "no gardening is as expensive as bad gardening, and the neglect of composts has ever been one of the characteristics of the negligent or bad gardener."

Paul next devotes two letters to the selection and arrangement of trees, evergreens, and flowering shrubs. In following letters he writes on the "American Garden" (a section of the property devoted to rhododendrons, mountain laurels, azaleas, magnolias, and other species native to the United States) and on the rose garden where, if there is not room for a *rosetum* made up of a several beds, "a single clump on a lawn is in good taste, formed either of standards or dwarfs, or of both combined." Then follows a letter on flowers in which he informs the reader, "What is termed 'CARPET BEDDING' is now becoming fashionable, and has been carried out with great skill and taste in the public parks of London." Here Paul adds the caveat that "this style of gardening is more elaborate and costly than gardening with ordinary bedding plants." In his next letter, "On Glass Structures," he maintains, "Although a greenhouse is not a necessary accompaniment to a garden, it yet adds greatly, and in a variety of ways, to its delights." Divided into two compartments, the warmer one will allow for the propagating and forcing of plants "to enliven the drawing-room or Conservatory in winter and early spring," while the cooler will serve to winter over tender plants such as fuchsias, geraniums, and camellias. The heated conservatory, usually an appendage to the house, is where the plants propagated and grown in the greenhouse are displayed "for the delight of the inhabitants when they have arrived at the proper size and are in their blooming season."

The letter "On Sweet-scented Plants and Flowers" enumerates the fragrant outdoor plants such as honeysuckle, jasmine, lavender, rosemary, sweet bay, sweet peas, violets, and roses, as well as less hardy ones such as cyclamen, daphne, heliotrope, hyacinths, narcissuses, night-scented stock, and sweet-scented verbena, which are grown in the greenhouse. In "The Fruit Garden," in which Paul discusses grafting, pruning, espaliering, pot cultivation, and how to construct a vinery, he writes, "If you desire [to produce really good grapes] you must employ a good gardener and leave the matter in his hands; it is therefore unnecessary that I should enter further here into details of cultivation." Following "The Vegetable Garden," he has four letters devoted to each season of the year, in which the gardener's tasks are outlined and an occasional tip offered. For instance, in the letter "Gardening in Summer" he advises, "If insects trouble you [in the fruit garden], dust the trees with snuff; and if they do not yield to this treatment, syringe them with soap-suds." Other letters cover the subjects of propagation, window gardening, plants suitable for children to grow, and the kinds of plants to grow in a shrubbery screen. His concluding letter is "Select Lists of Ornamental Trees, Fruit Trees, Shrubs, Flowers, Etc.," a helpful compendium of plants identified by both their Latin and common names.

An appendix provides a monthly calendar of operations,

enumerating the gardener's specific tasks throughout the year. The final pages of the book consist of the following advertisement: "WM. PAUL & SON avail themselves of this opportunity of inviting the attention of Amateur Horticulturists and others to the NURSERIES at WALTHAM CROSS (Eleven miles North East of London), which are open to the Public free daily (Sundays excepted)." There follows an itemization of the plants to be found in the Nursery Department, the Greenhouse and Florist Department, the Seed Department, and the Bulb Department. A concluding quotation from the *Journal of Horticulture* of April 9, 1868, provides the nursery with an imprimatur of the highest order: "On Thursday last, the 2nd of April, HER MAJESTY, accompanied by PRINCESS CHRISTIAN and PRINCE LEOPOLD, visited Mr. WM. PAUL's Spring Show at the Royal Horticultural Gardens, and, on inspecting the flowers, HER MAJESTY was graciously pleased to express her gratification and requested to be furnished with copies of Mr. PAUL's works on horticulture, which were at once supplied."

There could hardly be a clearer window through which to view Victorian gardening practice than the one Paul has opened for us in *The Hand-Book of Villa Gardening*. Read alongside Downing's *Treatise*, we gain an even clearer sense than before of the difference between England with its tradition of royal and aristocratic patronage and its long gardening history and America as a young nation striving to reinvent its English landscape heritage within the context of a newly prosperous republican society.

Foragers in the Garden
❦

XPLORATION, plant discovery, botanical science, and the introduction of new species into
cultivation was a vast and well-capitalized endeavor in eighteenth- and nineteenth-century
England. In that period, when imperial ambition made many
parts of the globe colonial provinces of the island-nation, British botanists were able to roam the world. On Captain Cook's
famous voyage to the South Seas of 1768–71, Joseph Banks
(1743–1820) collected seeds of many hitherto-unknown plant
species. As the most eminent British scientist of his day and
King George III's official advisor, Banks made botany one of the
Royal Academy's foundational disciplines. During the many
decades that he presided over this seminal scientific institution,
he sponsored numerous other naturalists on their voyages of
discovery. In the process he was able to oversee the transformation of the Royal Gardens at Kew into the world's foremost
botanical garden. Because of these synergetic activities, many
novel species were propagated and subsequently acquired by
large landowners and cultivated in the nation's private estate
gardens during and after Banks's lifetime. These plants and the
hybrids propagated from them vastly extended the botanical
palette. In the process, horticulture became an enterprise of

specimen display, giving rise to the challenge of combining native and exotic plants within a unified garden design.

In the nineteenth century America established its botanical counterparts to Kew, and the Arnold Arboretum and New York Botanical Garden sponsored expeditions by plant hunters to Asia and other faraway lands. However, many of the relatively young nation's own botanical riches were still new to cultivation both at home and in Europe, where they enjoyed the status of exotics. Rhododendrons and mountain laurel, originally discovered in the acidic soil of North American forests, entered the garden this way. Canada mayflower, Virginia creeper, trilliums, the delicate lady's slipper, and many more American wildflowers, a host of ferns, and numerous species of cacti, appreciated in their native habitats, were often dug up and naturalized in gardens. Wresting wild plants from their native ecological niches, a pursuit enthusiastically embraced at one time by ordinary gardeners and adventurous botanists alike, is of course a questionable practice in these more environmentally conscious days.

Reginald Farrer

Reginald Farrer (1880–1920) was one of that Banksian breed of intrepid plant explorers who scoured the recesses of the globe seeking hitherto-unknown specimens to bring into cultivation. Farrer's travels were directed toward the discovery of alpine plants, and he became the acknowledged doyen of rock gardening. Indeed, Farrer can be credited with transforming the alpine garden from Victorian trophy status into a special form of naturalistic horticulture. In his case, the objective was not so much garden design per se as the collection and cultivation of rare alpine plants under the appropriate set of topographic and soil conditions.

This was not easy. It demanded a keen knowledge and ability to reproduce, to the extent possible, the ecological conditions of the original mountain habitat of these delicate, finicky plants, something Farrer was singularly well-equipped to do. His family's estate, Ingleborough in north Yorkshire, boasted a limestone cliff overlooking a lake. This fissured karst formation offered as close an approximation as any geologic situation in England to the conditions conducive to growing alpine plants. From childhood, when he had precociously mastered a great deal of botanical science, this was Farrer's laboratory. But like other botanists of his day, what obsessed him was exploration to find species unknown to domestic horticulture. In spite of not being able to get institutional or commercial funding, he nevertheless managed to finance several Himalayan plant-collecting expeditions.

Even more opinionated than Robinson, in his several books—*My Rock-Garden* (1907), *Alpines and Bog-Plants* (1908), *In a Yorkshire Garden* (1909), *Among the Hills: A Book of Joy in High Places* (1911), *The Rock Garden* (1912), *On the Eaves of the World: A Botanical Exploration of the Borders of China and Tibet* (1917), and his magisterial, encyclopedic, two-volume work, *The English Rock-Garden* (1919)—Farrer praised the beauty of certain plants with unabashed ardor and snobbishly disparaged others. His literary voice, at once confident and confidential, is lushly vivid in its descriptive powers. A wild Mouton tree peony "carried at the top, elegantly balancing, that single enormous blossom, waved and crimped into the boldest grace of line, of absolutely pure white, with featherings of deepest maroon radiating at the base of the petals from the boss of golden fluff at the flower's heart." This observation was made from his vantage point on a hillside in Kandu Province in northwestern China.

Like collectors in other fields, the thrill of the chase and the sweetness of discovery is what motivated Farrer, who did not have to go to the Alps or remote Himalayas in order to search for novel treasures. *In a Yorkshire Garden* contains a passage in which he describes a rewarding foray much closer to home:

> I must tell you now . . . of a great joy that will always signalize this year in my memory. For the last decade I have diligently hunted through every wood of wild Anemones I passed, on the chance of finding the blue variety. For, be it known, whatever be the genuine nativeness of *Anemone apenniana, Anemone nemorosa* does undoubtedly, in the western parts, sport into various cerulean forms, and ultimately into that most bold beauty, *Anemone robinsoniana.* So, as I say, for years and for years had I hunted these blue forms, thinking that life could not possibly hold a joy more keen than the happening upon one. However, all my search was perennially useless. The best I ever achieved was a variety that took dull rosy tones as it faded—really quite an ordinary undistinguished thing.

The ecstatic moment came when, staying with a friend "who owns a very beautiful garden, in a glade of the hills,

"*Gentiana Acaulis* and *Draba Dediana*." Frontispiece and title page,
The Rock Garden by Reginald Farrer, 1912.

where every sort of beauty seems to thrive," the two went
looking for this desired treasure in a close-by wood as dusk
was falling. Farrer relates:

> We found a copsy hillside, dense with brushwood. I had been
> afraid the Anemones would all have shut their faces and gone
> to bed; but I soon saw that they were still clearly discern-
> ible. . . . I hunted on, heartened by occasional shouts from
> my friend, as he found a variety of more pronounced tone.
> And at last we came together (as we had only the one trowel
> between us) to collect an Anemone that really had the full ex-
> quisite lavender of *robinsoniana*, though with rather more blue
> in it. That was the moment, if you like! The culmination of
> years. There, in the silent gloaming, amid the serried spindly
> trunks, I reflected upon my prey and felt complete. And then,
> as I rose with the root in my hand, and still stooping, gave a

searching glance all round amid the bushes—(for, the nearer
you are to the ground, in such copses, the more clearly can
you scan the beds of flowers, the view being less impeded)—I
suddenly clutched my companion's arm, and pointed, inar-
ticulate. For there, rambling round a little tree, was a colony
of wood-Anemones bluer than any Anemone I have ever yet
seen in my life, excepting only *apennina* herself. Blue, blue, blue,
melting, cerulean, altogether exquisite and desirable.

In a frenzy of excitement, Farrer collects on until the
fall of complete darkness, cursing himself that he has not
brought a basket and has only a large handkerchief in which
to carry his booty. Returning to the magical copse the following morning, he finds the anemones "a blaze of starry
loveliness such as no painter would imagine in England."
Clambering uphill and then working his way down through
furze and thorns into a ditch, he looks up to behold a whole
slope covered with white wood-Anemones, glaring "with
an intense radiance like the white light that beats upon a
throne." Pressing on he finds yet another Anemone wholly
new to him, which he gathers up along with "more blues
cowering under a Holly-bush." When his basket is full to
overflowing he starts back only to be lured up "through the
brambles into the copse again, by the sight of some cerulean
or roseate star of Anemone among the tree-roots."

Upon his return home, Farrer planted the specimens from
the precious haul in his rock garden "in a choice corner made
for their special benefit," placing them in "pure leaf-mould,
and nothing else at all, to a depth of eighteen inches." But
this is not the end of the story. In his glasshouse he cross-

pollinates some of the anemone species, "For what a pride it would be to breed new races amid these beauties! And what a saving!"

As we have seen, soil quality is ever the true gardener's first consideration. Some plants require almost pure organic matter, others the opposite. In *In a Yorkshire Garden* Farrer devotes an entire chapter titled "The Old Moraine" to what he proudly claims to be "quite the most important discovery ever made as to the culture of Alpine plants in England." You can create this medium, which "costs literally nothing . . . by merely taking out so much soil from a bed or border, and then filling up the whole with fine road-metal and a little dust or soil." Simple. About his own moraine, he brags:

> I made it all with my own two hands, and I do sincerely contemplate the result and find it good. Four big blocks of limestone were . . . arranged in a hollow square, with a well at their centre. Some sharp, large rubbish was put in for drainage, and then the whole filled in with chips of blue limestone, such as they use in these parts for mending roads. And with a faint adulteration only, of soil.
>
> And then, by so happy a chance were those rocks adjusted, that when the moraine was made flush with the surface, the whole thing appeared at once as one enormous boulder, powdered with debris, in which it seemed a miracle that anything should live or find root-room. Down below, at the feet of the rocks, into joins and crevices, there nestle, at this day, big masses of mossy Saxifrage, Silver Saxifrage, Campanula and *Geranium lancastriense*. . . .
>
> And now, one final word before we leave this old and very delectable little moraine. In my own mind I attribute part of

its success to the super-excellence of its drainage. . . . And this is yet another comfort for those who want a little moraine, such as I have described, composed inside what looks like one great solid boulder; not only does this give you a compacter small garden, closer under your eye, and more isolated from everything else, but also it enables you to have it very well drained. . . . I could not desire, in the world, a more felicitous place for the growing of rare and delicate and difficult rock-plants.

Farrer's name ranks high in the rolls of garden writers whose books convey such authoritative advice that they are regularly consulted by other gardeners. This is true in part because rock gardening is a highly specialized form of horticulture, and his complete mastery of it has never been challenged. Even in the less-congenial gardening climate of the northeastern United

"*Saxifraga Gloria* (white) [*Saxifraga burseriana* 'Gloria'] and *S. Oppositifolia.*" *My Rock-Garden* by Reginald Farrer, 1907.

States, we find Louise Beebe Wilder citing him in *Adventures in My Garden and Rock Garden*. Speaking of how to coax into bloom a particularly delicate and beautiful primrose, she says "Even rumours of unreliability do not dim the pleasures of anticipation in this case, and one may hope by giving it good culture, a sheltered position in deep vegetable soil and grit, and, by the advice of Mr. Farrer, yearly division after flowering, to make it a permanent resident."

E. A. Bowles

*I*n his preface to his friend E. A. Bowles's (1865–1954) *My Garden in Spring* (1914), Reginald Farrer extols the author's garden in Middlesex near the Hertfordshire boundary: "Here are no precious plants pining for company in a grim and tidy isolation; here are no venerable ancient persons perpetually picking weeds until all the soil between every plant is bald as a billiard ball." High-flown language indeed, but not surprising when Farrer focuses on Bowles's rock garden, which appears to him to be "quite the finest piece of real gardening that I know . . . a roughly triangular piece of ground . . . surfaced and crammed and overflowing with rare Crocus and Primrose and Bland Anemone, and every vernal bulb that is usually looked after and cleansed and cosseted, but here left alone to make itself a wild plant and seed and establish in perfect naturalness under the eye of the gardener who knows and loves each one as a shepherd knows his lambs."

Like Farrer's Yorkshire garden, Bowles's was furnished with numerous rare plants gathered on forays into the wild rather than specimens grown in the nursery. He obviously fell into the category of those who possess "an inexplicable knowledge and feeling, [enabling them to receive] a sort of wireless message from the plant to the invisible antennae of the gardener. . . . Such a one sits down to unpack a box of novelties and can divide them out—Trilliums to the left-hand basket for the cool border, *Viola bosniaca* to the right for the sand-moraine, with *Wahlenbergia gracilis* and *Leucocrinum montanum* for companions."

Here is Bowles giving an imaginary tour of his garden in the spring:

I wish I could show you the Crocus frame and the seed-beds on a sunny morning in early February, that you might see these gems in the flesh instead of through this printed page. Let us be childish enough to 'make believe' we are doing it. I will take my garden basket and all its contents, almost as varied a collection as Alice's White Knight had, but certainly more useful, even the mouse-trap on too frequent occasions, while the cook's forks to extract new treasures, and painted wooden labels to mark them withal, are indispensable. It is noon, for I have waited for you, my visitors, and your train was late, delayed by fog in town which here was only a rime frost and white mist that the sun has conquered, and the lawns are only dewy now in the shadows, so we can take the short cut over them, passing the Snowdrop clumps and Aconite carpets and hurrying on to make the most of the sunshine, over the New River by the bridge guarded by the weird lead ostriches, which are six feet high and give some visitors a turn when they first see them. Into the kitchen garden, and don't look at the peach-house Crocus clumps yet, but hurry along past the vineries round by the stove and then—are they open? Yes, even in the seed-beds in the open air bees are busy on the lines of colour. There are several lines of uniform lilac—without a break of a pure white or deep purple original-minded babe; the labels at their heads tell us they are *Sieberi* or *Tomasinianus*, while solid yellow families are proclaimed as *ancyrensis*, *Korolkowii*, or *aureus*, but the variegated lines are our objects of veneration, where white, cream, sulphur-yellow, and lilac look as if all the seeds of the season had been mixed. The label on one such will perhaps say *chrysanthus* good white, another *c. pallidus*, or even striped seedling, but except those labeled *c. superbus* there is no uniformity, thank Heaven.

Bowles then goes on to provide the reader with helpful distinctions and detailed descriptions of these and several other crocus varieties. In the following chapter, with mounting excitement, he leads us to his rock garden to admire several other "early comers." "No one," he says, "would read a gardening book nowadays that did not deal with this latest fashion in gardening. The name and popularity and prattle of the thing are new, but many good cultivators had their porous, gritty, raised or sunk beds for alpines, whatever they called them, long ago." According to Bowles, the transformation of rock gardening into an art was due to Farrer's genius:

Then arose the prophet. The abundant rainfall of Ingleborough and the local limestone (three or four lumps of which make any sort of rock gardening a thing of beauty if only one side of the block be bedded up with earth), aided and abetted by river silt from the lake's mouth and chips of all sizes from the mountain side, were only waiting for Mr. Farrer's master mind to plan their combination and lo!

a new era dawned. The most discontented alpine treasures flourished, the great news went forth to the world, a series of books in slate-coloured covers became the foundation of conversation, even at dinner, to the great annoyance of those who wait and therefore should expect all things to come to them.

Bowles explains that while natural moraine ridges provide the ideal growing conditions for alpine plants, artificial ones can be constructed of other loose, rocky material. Not surprisingly, he is an enthusiastic convert to Farrer's method of making "Old Moraine." He confides, "Of course I was an early victim of the moraine measles after my first visit to Ingleborough, and when next the Moraine Magician came to see me, he helped in planning my first attempt at a granite chip [rock garden]," after which he explains how he experimented with different admixtures of rubble, stone, soil, peat, and sand to achieve the ideal and varied sets of conditions for growing different kinds of beautiful "early comers."

Bowles devotes a whole chapter to Alpine Primulas in which he narrates how he overcame his former aversion to these flowers. "But a few weeks among them in Tyrol, with Mr. Farrer as interpreter of their charms, converted me, and he likes to remind me of my declaration that I should not collect more than two or three of each and the contradictory reality of the full tins I carried on my poor old back down the mountain sides." Upon returning home, he pulled the roots of his plant clumps apart and set the separate rosettes in pure sand and leaf mold in a greenhouse. The next autumn he planted them in "an overgrown portion of the rock garden, hitherto sacred to Geranium species, [which] was torn down and rebuilt to imitate the Tyrolean homes from which I had exiled my Primulas." Growing ecstatic he tells how "*P. Juliae*, the new comer from Trans-Caucasia, has behaved here as a real lady, just as the bearer of such a name should. Two tuffets came from Herr Sündermann early in the year, their canary-coloured labels the showiest part of them. Cosseted for a little in a frame and then put out in cool, leafy soil they flowered brilliantly in late April. The astonishing crimson-purple of their flowers is in such sharp contrast with the brilliant yellow eye that every one exclaims 'Oh!' 'Marvelous!!' 'My stars!!!' 'Crikey!!!!' or something else according to the richness of their vocabulary, when they first see it."

My Garden in Spring can be considered part of a trilogy, for Bowles followed it with *My Garden in Summer* (1914) and *My Garden in Autumn and Winter* (1915). By means of additional imaginary garden tours during these seasons he gives the reader lively, fact-laced descriptions of the several varieties of peonies and roses in his summer beds and the different kinds of hardy chrysanthemums and Michaelmas daisies growing in great drifts in his fall borders.

Bowles has a particular fondness for geraniums. He tells us:

My interest in Geraniums dates from the day when as a small boy in a sailor suit I gathered a bunch of the Penciled Crane's-bill, *G. striatum*, in a lane near Paignton, and carried them to be named by my great-aunt, who was at once the central attraction and cause of our visit to South Devon, and the representative of all botanical lore to my young mind.

I owe so much to this delightfully clever and generous

Nature-lover that I cannot resist this opportunity of paying a tribute of gratitude to her memory. Mrs. Solly, my great-aunt Cornelia, had spent many years in India, and could tell tales and show wonderful drawings of plants and butterflies from "The Jungle" to the eager questioning child; but above all I recall happy sunny mornings passed with her in that wonderful Devonshire garden. I expect it was very small, but it seemed to me to contain everything worth growing, and I still believe its double Ranunculuses and Sparaxis and Ixias were the finest I have ever seen. Dear kind soul! How I hope there are sweet flowers in plenty round your feet in Paradise. . . .

Why do I like [Geraniums] so much? Let me think. Firstly, because of their name. Geranion is the old Greek name used by Dioscorides, and derived from *geranos*, a crane, because of the likeness of the unripe seed-vessels to the head and beak of that bird. Tournefort, and after him Linnaeus, used it to include the plants afterwards placed in two separate genera by L'Héritier, who seems to have invented the name of Erodium, from *erodios*, a heron, for the one, while for the other he adopted the name Pelargonium, from *pelargos*, a stork, first proposed by Dillenium in the *Hortus Elthamensis* in 1732 because he says Geraniums were called Stork-schnabel in Germany. . .

And on he goes in his discourse citing other botanical authorities throughout history.

The geranium in its several varieties was the summer successor to the spring bulbs in Bowles's rock garden. And summer, of course, is the time to go rambling about the countryside to see it growing in the wild. It is also the time visit other gardens and get new ideas from their owners. It is for this purpose that we find Bowles as the guest of a famous garden writer whom we have previously met:

> One hot July day, when I was staying with Mr. Robinson at Gravetye, I watched the seeds of *G. Lancastriense* being shot out, catapult fashion, by the drying and recurving slings formed by the beaks of the carpels, and as they were easy to collect from the grey flag-stones on to which they were falling I gathered a little pinch to pocket and carry off home to imitate the charming effect my host had achieved by using it as an edging to one of his beds, the rosy flowers looking especially lovely against the grey stones, and its tufty habit being just right for the position.

From reading Bowles we can conclude that plants are nature's great opportunists, seeding themselves wherever they can find a suitable niche in which to thrive we realize as well that avid gardens are also opportunists, ever on the lookout for new species to collect and install in their adopted homes. The fun of this lies not only in the delight of acquisition of new botanical curiosities but also in the embellishment of old parts of the garden and the creation of new areas where the plant collector's botanical treasures can be admired. Indeed, the saddest word for a true gardener is "finished." It is in the making and remaking that a garden remains alive; without the gardener's passion to incorporate new plant varieties and to redesign the garden in pursuit of a never-quite-achieved dream of perfection, it will become merely an exercise in routine maintenance or else suffer the all-too-common fate of neglect and oblivion.

"Hollyhocks, Sunflowers, and Eryngiums." *My Garden in Summer* by E. A. Bowles, 1914.

"I have a great weakness for single Hollyhocks and a dislike for ear-wiggy double ones, and a row of the former type, at the back of one of the Iris beds by the river, is a very fine sight, and is confirming me in my opinion that they are better than the double ones for this garden. They sow themselves, and provide endless variation of colour, and, if an especially beautiful one appears, it can be propagated by division. I will not say they are quite as immune to the rust as I at one time hoped, but they are certainly freer from it than any double forms I have tried."

"Hardy Chrysanthe-mums."
My Garden in Autumn and Winter by E. A. Bowles, 1915.

"In this garden the outdoor Chrysanthemums are crowded out of beds and the warm borders under walls they would like best, by tender shrubs and delicate plants dearer to my botanical mind. So they are grown in rows in the kitchen garden. And how delightful it is to walk in among them on a sunny morning, flower scissors in hand, to fill a basket with golden-orange Horace Martin, white and cream Mme. Desgranges, and Goacher's Crimson. This last is wonderfully good for cutting; but then so is Bobby, a brown pompon of delightful habit and staying powers. Cecil Wells is the best brilliant yellow I have found; Espérance, a good white, and Harvest Home a useful variety in which there is a mingling of bronze and red that goes well with other colours."

Herbert Durand

*L*ike gardens, the physical fate of books is as uncertain as the mortality of their former owners is certain. When the house is sold and emptied, who knows where the contents of the library are likely to end up? But then who knows where and what delightful finds from these same shelves a book collector may discover and add to her library one day? As in the case of William Paul's obscure catalogue, I was delighted to stumble upon another small gem, *My Wild Flower Garden* (1927) by Herbert Durand (1859–1944), which my son-in-law picked up from one of those sidewalk tables where secondhand books are sold and gave me as a Christmas present a few years back. It has a pretty orange dust jacket, its paper crumbling at my touch, and presumably was once given to someone by Mrs. Isaac LaBoiteaux of Bryn Mawr, since her calling card is tucked between its front endpapers. I ascertain from the preface written by the editors of *House & Garden* that the chapters first appeared as articles in the magazine. Perusing the book's contents makes it apparent that Durand was almost as keen a plant forager as Farrer, but instead of the Alps and Himalayas, he had the woods, meadows, and stream banks of suburban New York City as his happy hunting grounds.

Durand's purpose in writing *My Wild Flower Garden* was to demonstrate how, with a modicum of botanical knowledge and attention to horticultural requirements, the amateur gardener can turn a piece of unpromising ground into a beautiful rock garden. Like his British counterparts, Durand dwells on the importance of soil and the necessity of amending it in order to establish species-specific ecological niches that replicate as closely as possible the conditions of the sites where the wildlings were gathered. Like them, he must use considerable ingenuity in order to make his own wild flower garden look as naturalistic as possible.

We are introduced to this garden-making enterprise at its inception as Durand places soil of just the right degree of acidic, neutral, or alkaline composition and just the right amount of friable texture and organic admixture into the fissures and crevices of a large rock outcrop in order to transform sixty by one hundred feet of stony barrenness into a flourishing, plant-filled, miniature landscape. We learn how he obtains his plants by going on weekly collecting expeditions in the summer, mostly "from easy walking distance of my home." Here we must pause with a regretful sigh in light of our present-day knowledge of subsequent urban sprawl when he tells us, "I live barely three miles beyond the northern boundary of Greater New York and only thirty minutes from Broadway," adding this now-untenable generalization: "Abrupt transitions like this, from high brick walls and concrete pavements to virgin forests and fields untouched by the plow, are still characteristic of the environs of most American cities."

Environmental preservationists will take at least some comfort from knowing that "as one who realizes the urgent need of doing everything that is possible and practical to save, protect, and propagate our vanishing wild flowers, I must confess that I am sometimes conscious of 'that guiltiest feeling' while on distant collecting trips, particularly when some choice specimen is encountered that I know to be on the musn't pick lists of the preservation societies." Nevertheless, in some instances guilt can be overcome; Durand rationalizes:

> I have no compunction about digging any wild plant that will grace my garden if it is growing where new streets are under construction, building lots are about to be laid out and utter extinction of all wild life is imminent. That is an act of charity, like rescuing a homeless waif from the perils of the slums and giving it the shelter and comfort of a kindly household; for no plant goes into my garden unless a place is ready to receive it in which everything needful for its prosperity and safety has been provided.

Durand categorizes the kinds of flowers and ferns found both in the forest and in open country. "On banks [of woodland brooks] where the soil is rich and moist, but not really wet, spring beauties, trout-lilies, the dewdrop or dalibarda, the toothworts, anemones, and jack-in-the-pulpits mingle with lady ferns, New York ferns and interrupted ferns." By contrast, on dry, sandy hillsides and in fields, "many of the most showy wild flowers make their homes in dry, infertile soil, among them the yellow star grass, field or mouse-ear chickweed, wild indigo, blue lupine, bittersweet (on bushes and fences), birdfoot and arrow-leaved violets, butterfly weed, frost flower, sundrops, spreading dogbane, bergamot, blazing star, all the everlastings, showy goldenrod, blackeyed Susan, double-bristled aster, and golden aster." (A helpful index provides Latin as well as common names and page references.)

A chapter on "Digging, Packing and Replanting" instructs us on what to take for a short foray within walking distance: "An ordinary market basket, a twenty-five cent all-steel trowel, a pair of old scissors and a copy of the morning paper." Durand reminds "those unfortunates who are unable to tell one flower from another" to bring "a good wild flower book, of convenient pocket size, with accurate descriptions and graphic illustrations, for identification purposes." He gives precise and detailed instructions on how to treat the flowers you have carefully dug and wrapped individually in newspaper (or in moss when you are going on extended train or motor expeditions). Once transported, it is essential to match soil and sun conditions to each specimen's requirements as you insert the plants in the particular garden niches

"A Plant Properly Dug, With Ball of Dirt." *My Wild Flower Garden: The Story of a New Departure in Floriculture* by Herbert Durand, 1927.

you have prepared. Forty-one black-and-white photographs, presumably taken by Durand, display his transplants at their peak of performance. There are several pictures of a woman—his wife?—demonstrating various techniques such as how to dig up a plant with a ball of dirt attached to it, the way to maneuver your trowel under the roots, how to wrap plants in newspaper, and so forth.

The fundamental mark of the true gardener, as we have previously observed, is a deeply sensuous relationship to soil. Durand is no exception: "In early spring, like all devoted gardeners, I love the warm brown hues and the pleasant perfume of newly turned earth. Especially do I enjoy the feel and the frangipani-like fragrance of woodland soil." He remarks, however, that, as spring gives way to summer and the soil dries out and appears to be nothing more than bare dirt, the wildflower gardener must resort to ground covers and live mulches. Three years of trial and error have prepared him to tell you which plants are reliable for this purpose. He believes that "the partridgeberry is the best and altogether loveliest all-round groundcover in existence because it is evergreen, fragrant when in bloom, and always daintily attractive in any soil and cares not a whit whether it be located in deep shade or full sun." The wild gardener has several other ground cover options: "the little thyme-leaved speedwell, a denizen of low, wet, mucky or grassy places, is a perfect gem as a cover," bluets spread rapidly, and "the foam flower makes a charming carpet for a damp to moist, shaded or half shaded area where the soil is rich and the drainage is good." In addition, "the surpassingly lovely wild blue phlox is an ideal carpet for a woodland floor, when colonized in large quantities."

There is a vertical as well as a horizontal dimension to the wild flower garden, so you also need to read the chapter titled "Decorative Native Climbers." Durand tells us that of the twenty-two species of grapevines, twelve are indigenous to the United States. His favorite is the fragrant riverbank grape, which sprawls over bushes and low-branched trees growing near water from Maine to West Virginia and west to North Dakota, Colorado, and Texas. Virginia creeper, trumpet vine, honeysuckle, and clematis are among the "fifty or more native climbers and clamberers of modest spread that have sufficient decorative value to warrant their introduction into our gardens." He further maintains that no wild or woodland gardener can afford to do without the bittersweet, with its clusters of orange and scarlet autumn berries, which can become indoor decoration in the winter.

When it comes to "Growing the Finicky Wild Flowers"—none of which "will do its best either in soil that is intensely acid or in soil that has even a trace of lime"—he once more pricks the conscience of the reader. He hopes "that what I have to say will be seen and heeded by some of those misguided wild flower lovers who are, unwittingly in most cases, aiding in the extinction of many of the choicest and loveliest species. I refer to those transplanting zealots who, whenever they discover a flowering plant of unusual beauty in the woods or fields, are seized with an uncontrollable impulse to uproot it and carry it home." He points out that such treasures can usually be purchased from nurseries. If for any reason, however, it seems necessary to take from the wild such shy and delicate plants as pink and yellow lady-slippers, birdfoot violet, lavender and gold double-bristled aster, trailing arbutus, and the white pond lily in order to have an otherwise unobtainable specimen in the garden, only unwavering adherence to his prescribed procedures for digging and transporting them, along with sharp attention paid to the exact ecological requirements of each of the nineteen species he proceeds to discuss, will result in success. As for the bog-dwelling, carnivorous pitcher plant that only grows in sphagnum moss, Durand's advice applies strictly to the most expert plant-collecting enthusiasts; amateur gardeners should "leave them undisturbed in their natural haunts for the delectation of chance visitors who will respect their aloofness. Otherwise the time seems not far distant when they will become as extinct as the dodo."

Travelers in the Garden
✧✧✧

LANT foragers are, by necessity, travelers. But there is another kind of garden writer who travels. These are the tourists who visit gardens seeking beauty and education. Their quest is usually motivated by historical and cultural interest. Sometimes their explorations of foreign gardens provide a means of gathering ideas for their own gardens back home. Conversely, there are the expatriate garden writers who tell us how they replicated in another climate elements of the gardens they had known in their native land. As often, however, these writers simply desire to communicate their critical observations and convey their personal reactions. Their works should not be considered guidebooks as such, but one can—as I have upon occasion—find them very profitable to read in this manner.

Edith Wharton

*I*n the case of the novelist Edith Wharton (1862–1937), travel for aesthetic pleasure inspired this kind of garden writing. In *Italian Villas and Their Gardens* (1904) she set out to make discriminating American travelers appreciate the romantic remains of Italian Renaissance gardens. The success of this

"The Pool, Villa d'Este, Tivoli." Illustration by Maxfield Parrish from *Italian Villas and Their Gardens* by Edith Wharton, 1904.

beautiful volume, which was illustrated by Maxfield Parrish, contributed the imprimatur of a great lady of letters to the creation of Italianate gardens by wealthy Americans in what is often called the Country Place Era.

In reading Wharton, one should remember that she did not see the great sixteenth- and seventeenth-century villa gardens she describes as their owners originally conceived them—humanist itineraries encoded with messages celebrating the power of popes and pride of great aristocratic families—but as serenely beautiful artifacts with the mellowness of age that made them, in her eyes, enchanting rather than symbolic. What she captures with great perspicacity is the garden as structure, one that thoroughly melds architecture with landscape:

> The traveller returning from Italy, with his eyes and imagination full of the ineffable Italian garden-magic, knows vaguely that the enchantment exists; that he has been under its spell, and that it is more potent, more enduring, more intoxicating to every sense than the most elaborate and glowing effects of modern horticulture; but he may not have found the key to the mystery. Is it because the sky is bluer, because the vegetation is more luxuriant? Our midsummer skies are almost as deep, our foliage is as rich, and perhaps more varied; there are, indeed, not a few resemblances between the North American summer climate and that of Italy in spring and autumn.
>
> Some of those who have fallen under the spell are inclined to ascribe the Italian garden-magic to the effect of time; but, wonder-working as this undoubtedly is, it leaves many beauties unaccounted for. To seek the answer one must go

deeper: the garden must be studied in relation to the house, and both in relation to the landscape. . . . The Italian country house, especially in the centre and the south of Italy, was almost always built on a hillside, and one day the architect looked forth from the terrace of his villa, and saw that, in his survey of the garden, the enclosing landscape was naturally included: the two formed part of the same composition.

Wharton may have been somewhat mistaken in thinking that the Renaissance Italian villa garden had no flowers when she extolled it as simply a work of green architecture, but her notions that garden structure is the primary element of good garden design and that house and garden should be considered in relationship to each other and to the larger landscape is one that garden designers in any age would do well to heed. At the Mount in Lenox, Massachusetts, the house and garden she designed beginning in 1902, she did not strictly hew to her own advice. Here, instead of an axial and symmetrical layout uniting house and garden in a single frame as was the practice in the Italian villa gardens she admired, she confined her Italianate garden of green hedges and stone walls to the base of the sloping lawn while planting an unrelated, large, parterre bed of roses and other flowers beneath the windows of her study. If wanting in terms of overall design coherence, the gardens at the Mount are nevertheless a reminder of the range of this great American novelist's enthusiasms and talents.

Sir George Sitwell

Wharton's British contemporary, Sir George Reresby Sitwell, 4th Baronet (1860–1943), was an antiquarian and aesthete who was part of the Anglo-American expatriate colony that bought and renovated neglected Renaissance villas near Florence in the early part of the twentieth century. Sitwell purchased Castello di Montegufoni in 1909, the same year he published *An Essay on the Making of Gardens*. Subtitled *A Study of Old Italian Gardens, of the Nature of Beauty, and the Principles Involved in Garden Design*, the book is essentially a brief for the rejection of the Picturesque. Like Reginald Blomfield, Sitwell looked to historical precedent for examples of the structured formality he put forth as the successor to the eighteenth- and nineteenth-century Picturesque style. Not surprisingly, his gaze was directed toward Italy rather than the formal, seventeenth-century gardens of his own country, as was Blomfield's, for along with Harold Peto he was England's most enthusiastic champion of the Italianate style.

On the Making of Gardens is more a "why" than a "how" treatise, a book of principles, not a collection of pieces of horticultural advice. Sitwell justifies his enterprise by saying:

> During the last few years several sumptuous volumes have appeared illustrating the old gardens of Italy, yet except for a few hints given by Mrs. Wharton in her most valuable and charming book, little or nothing has been said about principles. If the world is to make great gardens again, we must both discover and apply in the changed circumstances of modern life the principles which guided the garden-makers

of the Renaissance, and must be ready to learn all that science can teach us concerning the laws of artistic presentment.

In fervid prose that often reaches the heights of the lyrical
(some might say purple), Sitwell disposes of what he considers the formulaic sterility of the seventeenth-century French
garden. Charging Le Nôtre with stealing the art of garden
making from Rome and Florence, but leaving the poetry behind, he laments how "the scepter of taste and fashion passed
at length from proud Italy to gaudy Versailles." He deplores
the subsequent age of "Classical Decadence," as manifested
in the decline of garden design into Rococo frivolity. He
loathed equally the sentimental Romanticism that arose
as a reactionary response to Le Nôtre's austere geometries.
Crowding together "in a few acres all the mood-compelling
aspects of nature" was no answer, for "the whole theory of
the natural garden is absolutely unsound."

Drawing on his visits to more than two hundred Italian gardens, as well as on the writings of John Ruskin and William
James, Sitwell proceeds to describe and critically compare
the aesthetic virtues of their designs along with the psycho-
logical responses they evoke. In this regard, it is important
to remind ourselves that Sitwell, like Wharton, did not see
the gardens in the age when they were emblematic of papal
power and princely pride. Instead, the sites had become artifacts of the classical grown Romantic. He tells us:

These old Italian gardens, with their air of neglect,
desolation, and solitude, in spite of the melancholy of
the weed-grown alleys, the weary dropping of the fern-

fringed fountains, the fluteless Pans and headless nymphs
and armless Apollos, have a beauty which is indescrib-
able, producing upon the mind an impression which it is
difficult to analyze, to which no words can do justice.

Like Wharton, he must resort to the term "garden magic"
to convey their ineffability. In almost fairy-tale language he
seeks to describe the Villa d'Este:

> In all the world there is no place so full of poetry as that
> of Villa d'Este which formalist and naturalist united to de-
> cry. Driving past the little Temple of Vesta, high above
> the seething cauldron of the Anio, one is admitted through
> vaulted corridors and deserted chambers where faded fres-
> coes moulder on the wall to a stairway overhanging the
> garden. And the garden that lies in the abyss below, terrace
> after terrace looking out upon wooded mountain flank and
> far mysterious plain—surely Time has forgotten these gi-
> ant cypresses which lift from the gulf dark pinnacles of night,
> great rugged, gloomy-verdured spires; surely it is the gar-
> den of a dream? Behind one like a cliff rises a palace of ro-
> mance, vast, august, austere; a palace over which in a far-off
> age some mighty magician has thrown an enchanting spell
> of sleep. Sleep and forgetfulness brood over the garden, and
> everywhere from sombre alley and moss-grown stair there
> rises a faint sweet fragrance of decay. . . .
>
> On the left, the garden looks down upon grey-green ol-
> ives shot with silver in the sunlight, and upon a vine-clad
> pergola which clings like a spider's web to undulating slope
> and dell. Deep drifts of withered leaves have gathered on the
> stairways, the fountain basins are overgrown with maiden-
> hair or choked with water-weeds, the empty niches draped
> with velvety moss or tapestried with creepers. Descending

by weed-grown stair and crumbling balustrade, one reaches a gloomy alley where a hundred fountains gush into a trough beneath a line of mouldering reliefs. At the further end of the terrace, falling in great cascades like the folds of a Naiad's robe or the flash of a silver sword, the river leaps into the garden, to four great pools of troubled water, a jeweled belt which quivers in the sunlight with a mysterious, an amazing blue. Such is the garden in the sober daylight, but what it may be in the summer nights, when the breath of the ivy comes and goes in waves of drowsy perfume, and great white moths are fluttering about the fountains, and in the ilex arbours and gloomy alcoves there are strange mutterings, and deep-drawn sighs, and whispering voices, and flashes of ghostly white, I do not dare to say.

This kind of analysis of "garden magic" is indebted to the aesthetic principles enunciated in somewhat less florid prose by Ruskin in *The Stones of Venice* (1853). It also derives from a deep reading of William James's monumental *Principles of Psychology* (1890), which holds that the distinction between "the primary feeling of beauty, as a pure incoming sensible quality, and the secondary emotions which are grafted thereupon, is one that must be made."

Obviously, it would be impossible to replicate the "garden magic" of old Italian Renaissance gardens whose essential ingredient is poetic decrepitude wrought by neglect and age. This was not, however, according to Sitwell, a reason to forsake the principles of Italian Renaissance garden-making in the design of new gardens or the renovation of existing ones. "Nature," he says with a nod toward Ruskin, "should call the tune," adding with Romantic fervor that "the melody is to be found in the prospect of blue hill or shimmering lake, or mystery-haunted plain, the aerial perspective of great trees beyond the boundary, in the green cliffs of leafy woodland which wall us in on either hand." He thus holds, "Next to the choice of site, I would put the maxim that we must subordinate the house to the landscape not the landscape to the house. . . . But the first aim of the designer will always be to consult the genius of the place." Then aesthetics comes into play, for "in a garden, as elsewhere, Art has the power of selection, accentuation, grouping, and the removal of defects or superfluities, to intensify and surpass the beauty of nature, thus reaching the ideal."

Calling on James, Sitwell asserts, "Art has another function also: it is concerned not only with the scene but with the mind of the beholder, for more than half of what we see comes from the mind." Here then at last we have found the garden-magic of Italy, in the domain of psychology, which Sitwell characterizes as "that occult science which deals in spells, exorcisms and bewitchments, in familiar spirits, in malign and beneficent influences and formulas of alchemy; that dim untrodden under-world from which Shakespeare and Wagner drew their shadowy legions, which will yet inspire great poets, artists and musicians of the age to come."

Such were the underpinnings of the Italianate style as derived from fundamental theory rather than mere replication. In restoring, according to the principles he espoused, the gardens at Renishaw Hall in Derbyshire, his ancestral seat

"The Cortile." Frontispiece, *A Garden in Venice* by Frederic Eden, 1903.

whose castellated great house was built in 1625, Sitwell incorporated many of the elements he had deeply pondered in the Italian villa gardens of old. These included axial alleys lined with statues of mythological deities; stone urns, marble fountains, and other sculptural accents terminating vistas; an architectural framework of green, hedge-enclosed garden spaces; holly and camellia avenues; and geometrically clipped yews.

Sir George's son Osbert saw little garden magic in the place. According to him, "[My father] abolished small hills, created lakes, and particularly liked to alter the levels at which full grown trees were standing. Two old yew trees in front of the dining-room window at Reninshaw were regularly heightened and lowered; a process which I believe could have been shown to chart, like a thermometer, the temperature of his mood."

Frederic Eden

*F*rederic Eden (1828–1916) was, like Sitwell, an expatriate in love with Italy. However, instead of taking the principles of Italian garden-making back to England, he and his wife Caroline, the sister of Gertrude Jekyll, brought their taste for English gardens to Italy. Eden's *A Garden in Venice*, published by Country Life in 1903, is an account of their garden's creation. Like other garden lovers, I have stood longingly on a quiet *calle* on the Giudecca beside its iron gates, which have long been shut to even the most determined would-be visitor. One surmises that what lies on the other side are weeds and a general state of dereliction.

This was much the condition the garden was in when Eden bought the Palazzo Barbarigo in 1884. By then, the grounds had become a market garden filled with cabbages, artichokes, fruit trees, tangled vines, and collapsed arbors. There were broken statues and carved stone vases lying on the ground, and according to Eden, "sweetbrier, cabbage and moss roses, with iris and white lilies, their bulbs struggling for existence half out of the ground, seeking in the air the nourishment an exhausted soil could no longer give them."

The challenge was how to balance regard for "genius of place" with the couple's wish to have a garden similar to one they had known and loved in Ross-shire in Scotland. First, however, they had to deal with their degraded site:

One or two pergolas were suppressed where the vines were past recovery or weak, and one or two squares [of the current layout] were thrown together, thus in one case massing two tiny orchards . . . that looked at each other across the line of the vines they stifled. Workers were brought in to construct new pergolas and paths, and mindful of Hyde Park, boat-loads of sea shells were brought from the Lido as substitutes for, and improvement on, the gravel that the Veneto does not furnish. The paths were then bordered with box or old bricks. The last the best, for bricks, especially the old ones, are not unsightly, want no trimming, take nothing from the soil, harbor no insects, and hold rather than consume the precious moisture.

Then the borders were planted, not an easy task, for one side of the pergola running as ours mostly do, east and west, is in the shade. Sometimes too the pergolas are doubled to meet the exigencies of some extra vigorous vines, and few herbaceous and seedling plants will submit gracefully to be deprived of so much light and air. It took then some time to fill them, and it takes some thought to keep them filled, but nothing is more marvelous than the growth and multiplication of plants in Venice that are pleased with Venice. And here a word must be said on the peculiarities of Venice gardening, bound up, as these are with its pains and pleasures.

There is no other soil and climate so full of whim and fantasy. You buy a score of magnolias, trees that you see growing luxuriantly in other Venice gardens. One of your score alone will perhaps thrive. You plant a dozen roses of the same kind, bought from the same rose garden; this and that plant will ramp, the rest not move. Your efforts to fill the garden is a story of failures, and yet the successes thrive so fast that the scissors and knife and billhook must be kept at work to let in air and sunlight.

After a time our thick heads found out one cause of failure. The soil is made; brought in boats from pulled down houses or dust heaps, or from the bottom of dredged canals. One rose you plant may have the luck to light on an ancient dung heap, the next vainly strive to root in the scorched debris of some long-forgotten fisher's kitchen. Again, the soil on the surface may be sweet and wholesome, but all plants that have tap-roots, or seek deep feeding, would find at some three feet down salt earth or even salt water. I have seen in a very hot and dry summer the surface in places white with a salt efflorescence drawn up by the power of the sun.

In spite of the undependable soil, the Edens were able to proceed by trial and error and in the end achieve a flourishing and beautiful garden. Although they may have received advice on various plants from Caroline's sister Gertrude, they wished to avoid above all "the high priests of gardening, who, with dogmatic confidence, tell us what is wrong and what is right."

To make over the garden entirely was unthinkable. Their method was to respect the basically geometrical plan, while adding a few ideas gathered from nearby Italian gardens or such distant ones as the Generalife in Granada, at the same time keeping in mind the outlines of their fondly remembered Ross-shire garden. Thus:

One or two of the squares, formed in accordance with the Scottish design, were at once stolen from [the former caretaker's] vegetables and laid out in rose gardens. Year after year the same theft was made until we were obliged to stop; not for kitchen needs, or less love of roses, or from lack of other varieties to add to those we have, but that we thought, and think, the mixture of the useful with the beautiful gives the latter greater value. . . . Two other small lawns were made as the ground plan of some oleanders; one of these shrubs, not less than thirteen or fourteen feet in height, and as many in breadth, is, in July, one mass of bright red flower. Others are red and pink, or various tints, and pale yellow and pure white.

Round and on these lawns, too, are Japanese kaki, the only magnolia I can get to grow, and pomegranates. The kaki and the small Japanese maples are worth a place in any garden. The last are slow in growing; but the kaki shows more than mere contentment with its new home by the vigor of its growth, the masses of its beautiful glossy dark foliage, and the size and quantity of its luscious golden orange fruit.

Of the pomegranates we have several kinds. It is the common one that gives the fruit, so dear to old designers on wood and canvas, and in marble, stone, and metal. Other species have double flowers, red, red and white, and white; the first two grow luxuriantly and are beautiful. . . .

As the cabbages and artichokes of our prepossessors gave way to the daffodils, anemones, and tulips mostly bought from Holland, the produce of these bulbs yearly made demand for greater space. Small islets of foxgloves or columbines or larkspurs spread themselves into continents, and a splash of Love in the Mist flowed over into a sea of blue. The vigor, too, of the plants that love the soil is so great that to reduce them and their groups to the dimensions that are observed in what is called a well-kept garden would be to restrain their nature, and we mostly prefer to let them ramp. As much as possible we give Nature her head, and when she is ridden it is with the lightest snaffle.

It is clear from this description that the Edens' garden was a unique creation, a marriage of site and sentiment, of native growing conditions and foreign ideas, of indigenous vegetation and imported species. It was thus not a piece of Scotland in Italy but rather a fusion of Italy and Scotland, a piece of paradise in the world's most beautiful city.

Paula Deitz

*A*lthough she would not classify herself as an active gardener, Paula Deitz's (b. 1938) lively essays on various world landscapes can be read as bulletins from abroad, bringing news and ideas to those who are too busy at home minding their own gardens to travel. In *Of Gardens* (2010), a substantial omnibus of selected essays she has written over the course of the past thirty years, Deitz demonstrates her capability both as a garden guide and garden writer.

Deitz's literary stance falls into the category of "Letter from . . . ," the magazine piece that sounds like an epistolary account of a trip written to a friend who will recognize and enjoy the erudite references she makes in passing. Her use of allusion and simile is a way of placing the topic at hand in historical and cultural context. In both length and substance her essays are naturally tailored to suit the requirements of the various publications for which she writes. Among these are *The New York Times*, *Gardens Illustrated*, *Architectural Record*, *Vanity Fair*, *Antiques*, *Metropolis*, *Hortus*, and *Site/Lines*.

The pieces written for *The New York Times* are necessarily the briefest and most topical, as for example the archaeological discovery in 1985 of what was probably the earliest garden in America at Bacon's Castle, twelve miles south of Williamsburg, Virginia. Longer, less news-driven articles written for magazines and journals allow her propensity for imaginative associations to range more freely. But whether writing for the *Times* or one of several other periodicals represented in this collection, her subject is always linked to some kind of personal observation, for Deitz refuses to write about a place she has not visited, a person she has not interviewed, or an exhibition she has not seen. After establishing her on-site presence, she allows the reader's imagination to roam with hers as she makes fortuitous, sometimes surprising connections. Often these include references to other garden writers, such as Celia Thaxter and Gertrude Jekyll, and there are allusions as well to painters such as Thomas Cole and to authors such as Henry James, Sarah Orne Jewett, and Hans Christian Andersen.

For me, perhaps the finest essay in the book—one that Deitz wrote without the restrictions of deadline or word count—is her introduction to her book *The Bulletins of Reef Point Gardens* (1997). This piece stands on its own as an excellent short biography of Beatrix Farrand, an extraordinary garden designer and plantswoman as well as America's first important woman landscape architect. Farrand's bulletins document the results of the horticultural experiments and landscape studies she conducted at Reef Point, her six-acre garden in Bar Harbor on Mount Desert Island, Maine, where many of her clients also had summer residences. When at the age of eighty-two, Farrand saw that her plans to have Reef

Point perpetuated as a study center beyond her lifetime had become impractical, she made the difficult decision to sell the property. Stoic in the face of this necessary loss, she oversaw the gift of her twenty-seven-hundred-volume horticultural reference library—it included, along with several rare books, the archives of Gertrude Jekyll—to the library of the Department of Landscape Architecture at the University of California, Berkeley. The sorrow of dismantling the garden, which Farrand was determined to do rather than have it fall into ruin, was mitigated to a degree by the transfer of many of her finest trees and shrubs to the nearby Thuya Garden and the beautiful Asticou Azalea Garden created by the Asticou Inn's owner, Charles K. Savage, on the opposite side of the street.

Deitz brings us to the place where we can best comprehend the nature of Farrand's enterprise. Thus we find ourselves strolling with her along Bar Harbor's long Shore Path past several Maine "cottages" to the one that Farrand's parents had built in 1883. Although the property is now divided into five parcels, she tells us that "to all appearances, it is possible to walk to the end of Hancock Street in the silence of a summer afternoon and stand in front of the granite gate pillars and finials of Reef Point under towering white spruces as though nothing had changed." Beyond the gate, we will see that "a curved entrance drive leads to the picturesque Gardener's Cottage, one of the few buildings to survive the demolition of the gardens. A short stroll along the lichen-covered white cedar boundary fence on the Shore Path gives a sense of the dramatic views across the water, which determined the axes

of the fanned-out garden paths." Through felicitous compari-
son and vivid description, Deitz then makes us aware of Reef
Point's importance as a landscape:

> In the history of garden design, the influence of Reef Point
> Gardens as a personal expression of horticultural taste and
> design may be compared with such other pivotal gardens as
> Gertrude Jekyll's Munstead Wood and William Robinson's
> Gravetye Manor, both of which Farrand visited in England.
> It was modern in the sense that its design did not allude
> to any historical style but was instead an enhancement of
> an elaboration of the natural features of Maine, such as the
> native bunchberry (*Cornus canadensis*), for example, which
> grew in dappled sunlight at the entrance to a wood. But her
> gardens also possessed components necessary to a botanic
> garden: systematic classification of plants of a single species;
> an herbarium of almost eighteen hundred plants, created
> for scientific study; and micro-environments specific to the
> coast of Maine, such as a bog filled with purplish pitcher-
> plants. With the gardens charted into sections and the
> plants labeled, the scientific scope of Reef Point—yielding
> a disciplined design with its own harmonies of color, texture,
> and form—was akin to those early botanic gardens founded
> by professors and physicians at medieval universities.

Deitz then conducts us on Farrand's circuit of the now-
vanished garden, reconstructing its sequence of parts from
descriptions in the bulletins. Starting at the vine gardens
alongside the house, we follow in her footsteps as she reveals
for us the garden as it existed in Farrand's time. Passing beyond the rose gardens, we come to an area planted with rhododendrons and mountain laurels, following which we tour

the kitchen garden with its espaliered fruit trees, the perennial borders and rock garden facing one another across the lawn, the mass of pink azaleas, the holly hedges, the collection of heathers, and at last the bog garden with its intriguing, carnivorous pitcher plants. We learn that the remaining native spruces were part of an enclosing windbreak, and we can still see across the bay the pointed firs, memorably described by Sarah Orne Jewett, terminating the view from the garden in a serrated horizon line. Summoning Celia Thaxter to her side, Deitz compares the seemingly casual abundance of Thaxter's Appledore Island garden with Reef Point where Farrand "did what she loved most by creating a Maine garden of apparent simplicity where families of plants laid out in drifts meshed with others in a studied asymmetry."

While infectious enthusiasm is what drives Deitz's usual laudatory prose, she is a design critic capable of negative judgment as well as praise. Such is the case when she writes "A New Memorial Squanders a Sparkling Opportunity," an essay about the bombastic architecture of the World War II monument on the Washington Mall. Here, however, she does not merely deplore but also instructively compares this memorial with others that actually accomplish the difficult task of finding an appropriate architectural vocabulary to do justice to the sober task of commemorating sorrow and making victory something greater and more humanly significant than mere patriotic celebration. Thus, after remarking how "the characterless blocky surfaces of the memorial's structures and oversized open plaza radiate a blinding whiteness, particularly notable in Washington's humid summer heat," she directs our attention to Lawrence Halprin's Franklin Delano Roosevelt Memorial overlooking the nearby Tidal Basin and to the Lincoln Memorial at the terminus of the Mall. These monuments make evident the magnitude of the squandered opportunity: "Whereas the Roosevelt Memorial allows the visitor to think between inscriptions and episodes and the Lincoln Memorial offers the cool majesty of a Greek temple interior, here there is no relief from the onslaught of words and symbols." With such trenchant observations Deitz shows that the discerning eye and the sympathetic heart are essential organs for achieving a satisfying and resonant memorial design. We might ask ourselves, "Aren't those the requirements of every successful garden as well?"

Humorists in the Garden

❧❧

RATHER than instruct (Loudon), portray (Jekyll), proselytize (Robinson), rhapsodize (Thaxter), or serve as erudite travel guide (Deitz), some garden writers set out to entertain. They are not less passionate about their gardens or less obsessed with gardening, but they see in these very traits the stuff of comedy.

Reginald Arkell

*I*f Celia Thaxter's fierce nocturnal battle with loathsome slugs is a source of unintentional humor, novelist and playwright Reginald Arkell (1882–1959) makes this most detested of garden pests an outright subject of comic satire in *Green Fingers: A Present for a Good Gardener* (1936), the first of several charming books of light verse dealing with the gardener's joys and woes. Throughout, Eugène Hastain's amusing vignettes add their own note of levity to Arkell's lighthearted verse.

"Green Fingers"

This book is meant for people who
Can always make their gardens do
Exactly what they want them to;

Who search their borders every night,
And catch their slugs by candle-light;
Who always start at crack of dawn
To dig the plantains from their lawn;
Whose paths are always free from weeds;
Whose plants are always grown from seeds;
Who are most careful not to prune
That standard rose a day too soon;
Who are quite rude to men who sell
Tobacco plants that have no smell;
In fact, to all of you, I mean,
Whose fingers are reputed green
Because you keep your borders clean.

Here we meet up again with Celia Thaxter's foe as well as every other gardener's bane:

The Lady with the Lamp

There is a lady, sweet and kind
As any lady you will find.
I've known her nearly all my life;
She is, in fact, my present wife.
In daylight, she is kind to all,
But, as the evening shadows fall,
With jam-pot, salt and sugar-tongs
She starts to right her garden's wrongs.

With her electric torch, she prowls,
Scaring the Nightjars and the Owls,
And if she sees a slug or snail
She sugar-tongs him by the tail.
Beware the pine-tree's withered branch,
Beware the awful Avalanche—
And Slugs, that walk abroad by night,
Beware my wife's electric light.

And now see how another female gardener loses her gentility:

A Perfect Lady

I knew a girl who was so pure
She couldn't say the word Manure.
Indeed, her modesty was such
She wouldn't pass a rabbit-hutch;
And butterflies upon the wing
Would make her blush like anything.
That lady is a gardener now,
And all her views have changed, somehow.
She squashes green-fly with her thumb,
And knows how little snowdrops come:
In fact, the garden she has got
Has broadened out her mind a lot.

We could go on munching these wry garden crudités, but we'll stop here with Dame Vegetable:

The Lady of Shalots

Have you forgotten, Curly Head,
That night beside the Parsley Bed?"
"I have forgotten it," she said.
"Do you recall the word you spoke
That night beneath the Artichoke?"

"Oh, that," said she, "Was just a joke."
"Have you forgotten how you cried
Among the Onions?" I sighed.
"Well, do you blame me?" she replied.
I spoke of sympathetic scenes
Between the Parsnips and the Beans;
But when I called her my Shalot
And said what Celery I got—
She told me not to talk such rot.
Ah, Kitchen Garden, soaked in rain
I ne'er shall see her like again.

Yet Arkell is more than a garden versifier. In addition to his plays and other novels, he is the author of *Old Herbaceous* (1951), a tender portrait of a head gardener during the years that saw the transformation of English gardening from the scale that was practiced in the Edwardian era on great country estates to a much-diminished one following the social and economic changes wrought by two world wars. The affectionate humor with which he details the duties and personality of his charmingly crusty protagonist as he reflects on a long, mutually respectful relationship with his employer and the diminished importance he suffers with dignity as he observes from his pensioner's cottage window the changing standards of his profession has made this book a much-loved garden classic.

Karel Čapek

*C*zech patriot, playwright, and novelist Karel Čapek (1890–1938) reminds us of Jane Loudon in that he wrote of futuristic inventions, notably robots, in a manner that foreshadowed the genre of science fiction, not to mention some of the technological marvels we are witnessing today. The chapters in his enduring small classic, *The Gardener's Year* (1929), derived from his regular column in the newspaper *Lidové noviny*, are arranged according to the months. Here we find a series of humorous sketches in which the beleaguered gardener is pitted against nature, his necessary partner and unpredictable adversary. Čapek wryly enumerates his trials and tribulations as he is besieged by capricious weather, high winds, too hard a frost, too little rain, too much dry summer heat, a recalcitrant garden hose that sprays more of the gardener than the garden, and many similar frustrations and

indignities. In the chapter on January, for instance, Čapek asserts:

> The worst time for the gardener is when black frost sets in. Then the earth stiffens and dries to the bone, deeper day by day and night after night. The gardener thinks of the roots which are freezing in the soil, dead and hard like stone, of twigs benumbed to the pith by the dry, icy wind, and of freezing buds which the plant packed all its goods and chattels into in the autumn. If I thought it would help, I would dress my Holly in my own coat and put the Juniper in my own trousers. For you, Pontic Azalea, I would take off my shirt. You, Alum Root, I would cover with a hat. And for you, Tickseed, there is nothing left but my socks; you can make do with those.

A cartoon of the clothed plants by Čapek's older brother, Josef, a talented painter and set designer, accompanies this lament against the harshness of winter. Other similarly charming drawings by Josef, which perfectly complement Karel's comic prose, are sprinkled throughout the book.

As must all good gardeners, Čapek starts from the ground up with seeds and soil:

> [A gardener] lives submerged in the ground. He builds his memorial in a pile of compost. If he were to go to the garden of Eden, he would sniff intoxicatedly and say, 'There's humus here, by God!' I think that he would forget to eat the fruit of the tree of knowledge of good and evil; more likely, he would look to see how he could take away the odd wheelbarrowfull of the Lord's paradisiacal topsoil. Or he would discover that the tree of the knowledge of good and evil did not have a nice, bowl-shaped border fashioned round it and would begin to fumble about in the soil, not even knowing what was hanging above his head. 'Adam, where are you?' the Lord would call. 'In a moment,' the gardener would reply over his shoulder, 'I haven't got time just now.' And he would go on making his border.

Charles Dudley Warner

Like Čapek, Charles Dudley Warner (1829–1900) produced
My Summer in a Garden (1870) from contributions to a newspaper column and, like the Czech, the American used a dry wit
to fashion his gardener's persona. The collected pieces, which
were originally published in the *Hartford Courant*, are the stuff
of laughter, and Warner's book is another delightful garden
classic in which sprigs of moral philosophy sprout within the
garden's luxuriant beds.

No one reading the ponderous articles Warner wrote for
Harper's Magazine as a reporter on the affairs of the nation and
other weighty matters would have guessed that he was as capable of employing comic hyperbole as his next-door neighbor and close friend Mark Twain. Indeed, it was Warner, not
Twain (to whom it is universally attributed), who coined the
aphorism, "Everybody complains about the weather, but no-
body *does* anything about it."

Prefacing his book with a meditation on man's most basic
relationship with the earth, he writes:

> The love of dirt is among the earliest of passions, as it is
> the latest. Mud-pies gratify one of our first and best in-
> stincts. So long as we are dirty, we are pure. Fondness
> for the ground comes back to a man after he has run the
> round of pleasure and business, eaten dirt, and sown wild-
> oats, drifted about the world, and taken the wind of all its
> moods. The love of digging in the ground (or of looking
> on while he pays another to dig) is as sure to come back to
> him, as he is sure, at last, to go under the ground, and stay
> there. To own a bit of ground, to scratch it with a hoe, to

plant seeds, and watch their renewal of life,—this is the commonest delight of the race, the most satisfactory thing a man can do.

In addition to dwelling in satirical terms on the many torments inflicted by the striped bug, seed-filching birds, pecking chickens, moles, weeds, and more, Warner, who was a genial man and much-loved figure in Hartford, dons the mask of the exasperated curmudgeon in his mock tirade on the nuisance of children:

> The neighbors' small children are also out of place in your garden, in strawberry and currant time. I hope I appreciate the value of children. We should soon come to nothing without them. . . . But the problem is, what to do with them in the garden. For they are not good to eat, and there is a law against making away with them. The law is not very well enforced, it is true; for people do thin them out with constant dosing, paregoric, and soothing-sirups, and scanty clothing. But I, for one, feel that it would not be right, aside from the law, to take the life, even of the smallest child, for the sake of a little fruit, more or less, in the garden. [When we come to] join that innumerable caravan which moves [to the next world], it will be some satisfaction to us, that we have never, in the way of gardening, disposed of even the humblest child unnecessarily.

On behalf of the neighbors' children, we should be thankful that Warner's ironic forbearance prevailed. On our own behalf as readers, we should be grateful that Henry Beecher Stowe, the famous minister and brother of Warner's other famous neighbor, the author of *Uncle Tom's Cabin*, encouraged the publication of this engaging collection of garden pieces.

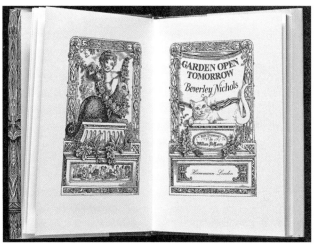

Frontispiece and title page, *Garden Open Tomorrow* by Beverley Nichols, with drawings by William McLaren, 1968.

Beverley Nichols

*I*t is as a purveyor of offbeat garden humor that Beverley Nichols (1898–1983), a popular British playwright, journalist, composer, and public speaker, is best remembered. His first book, *Down the Garden Path* (1932), is based on the garden he made next to his Tudor cottage in the small remote county of Huntingdonshire where, "if you go into its sleepy little capital and drink a bitter at one of the little inns, you will find farmers who speak with a dialect which would sound familiar to Pepys, who had a cottage in the neighborhood." Nichols's style is one of cheerful exaggeration, pleasant mockery, and droll similes. He is breezy and chipper, and we feel sometimes when we are in his company that P. G. Wodehouse might stop by for tea at any moment.

"Are you bored?" Nichols asks rhetorically after seven pages describing blue flowers in his winter garden. With liberal use of the pathetic fallacy, he continues:

> Indeed, I hope not. For the flowers' sake, not for my own. At the risk of out-winnying the poo, it must be admitted that I always think flowers know what you are saying about them. If I see a scraggly lupin, I like to pass well out of its hearing before delivering any adverse comments on it. For how do we know what tortures it may be suffering? It surely can be no more pleasant for a lupin to have to appear with tarnished petals than for a woman to be forced to walk about with a spotty face. One does not say, 'Oh look at that awful girl covered with pimples!' Why then, should one stand over flowers and hurl insults at them? Besides, the flowers' condition may be all your own fault, which cannot be said of the girl's complexion, unless she is a particular friend of yours and you have been keeping her up too late at night.

This empathy for plants was inherited. In a chapter titled "Miracles," he narrates:

> My father called to me from the garden.
>
> 'Here! Come out and look at this!'
>
> There was a note of urgency in his voice. I threw away the book I was reading, and hurried out. My father was standing in the little arbour which leads into the Secret Garden. I went to him, and looked.
>
> I do not know if one's heart ever really stands still, but mine at that moment stood as still as it is ever likely to do, until it stops forever.
>
> For there, underneath a tangle of ivy, sweet-brier, honeysuckle and jasmine, was a little bunch of grapes. True, the

grapes were green and not much larger than peas. But the bunch was perfectly formed, and it hung its head delicately, as though it were diffident that it had been discovered.

'Grapes!' I whispered.

'And how they're alive at all, beats me,' observed my father.

He had every reason to be surprised. The very survival of this vine was a miracle. For its roots were mixed up with those of a rank and greedy laurel. Its stem was being throttled and eaten by a rapacious ivy. Its slender branches were buried, tangled, and overcast by a thick roof of many creepers. Hardly a leaf of that vine can ever have seen the sun. Why, there was even a flourishing elm tree, high above the thicket, casting so thick a shadow that the sturdiest of the creepers had grown pale and anemic.

Add to all these things the fact that we had suffered the worst summer within living memory . . . a summer of endless rain and biting winds. . . .

Yet, in the cold and the darkness, in the face of fierce competition, the little vine had produced a bunch of grapes. If that is not a miracle, I should like to know what is.

After a spate of other books about gardens, including *Green Grows the City* (1939), about his later garden at Hampstead Heath, he wrote *Garden Open Tomorrow* (1968), this one set in a third garden, at Sudbrook Cottage in Surrey, where he moved in 1958. In this last book, with its charming chapter-head vignettes by William McLaren, he picks up his playwright's pen to give these stage directions:

Scene

The porch of the music-room. Through the windows one can see a moonlit lawn, still faintly streaked with snow.

Time

The small hours of a bitter morning in March.

Dramatis Personæ

Gaskin, in his accustomed role of factotum.

Four and Five, in their accustomed mood of *hauteur* and disdain, which they never fail to display when I return home after a long absence. Both are sitting very close to the fire with their backs squarely turned towards me. From time to time they glance at one another with meaningful expressions. 'This sort of thing,' they are saying, 'is becoming far too frequent. He seems to imagine that he can go away for months on end and then expect us to behave as though nothing had happened. He must not be allowed to get away with it. He must be *shown*.' And show me they do, in the most unmistakable manner. It will be nearly a week before they really relax.

Finally myself, a little dazed after jetting across the Atlantic, but itching to get into the garden in spite of the fact that it would really be more sensible to wait till dawn.

So I say good night and Gaskin picks up Four and Five in a single accomplished swoop. They dangle in front of him, a most alluring bundle of scorched fur, faintly powdered with wood-ash. I step towards them hoping that they will at least show some sign of recognition. I am greeted by two green, icy stares. I should have known better.

And now we can open the door of the porch and step outside.

Nichols uses similar humor to approach a more sober moral topic. In a chapter called "The Enemy Within Our Gates," he declares himself to be on friendly terms with the whole animal kingdom, hoping that "when one goes to heaven one will be constantly surrounded—indeed almost smothered—by furred and feathered creatures who will no longer be agitated by the fears that beset them on earth." He then slyly demurs, "But sometimes . . . well . . . I wonder."

He has, after all, to confront a plague of squirrels, the not-to-be-deterred predators who steal all the nuts from his walnut tree. He laments:

The squirrels have arrived, precisely on time. It is really quite extraordinary, as though they kept diaries in which they wrote: 'Sunday July 9. Call on B. N. and inspect walnut trees.' At the moment there are only two of them, a sort of advance guard, flicking their tails in the swaying branches;

"The Enemy Within Our Gates." Drawing by William McLaren, from *Garden Open Tomorrow* by Beverley Nichols, 1968.

and since they have not yet realized their strength, and still have some of the innate timidity of wild creatures, they scamper away at a clap of a hand, streaking from the walnut into the deeper recesses of the copper-beech, and from there into the pear tree, whence they disappear into one of the neighbouring gardens. But they will be back tomorrow, and the day after, and in ever increasing numbers, and for weeks the lawns and paths will be littered with scraps of shells and broken nuts, and the whole garden will look like Hampstead Heath after an exceptionally rowdy bank holiday.

Nothing to be done here. But now comes the real moral dilemma. The gardener may stay his hand as he sees "a woolly caterpillar having an expense-account luncheon off the leaves of a Super Star rose," imagining the caterpillar imagining it-self and its companion caterpillars ruminating as they chew. They are thinking of how, when summer comes, they will all be "safely and gloriously attired in the dresses that Nature is keeping in store for us, fluttering over these roses in the guise of butterflies." But such sentimental anthropomorphizing doesn't last long. Thinking of how his blighted roses will look come summer, Nichols admits that "before the day is out one will have visited the tool-shed to make sure that there is an adequate stock of poisonous insecticides with which to deal with the problem." Then in two sentences the essay pivots, as the author does an about-face: "There is only one drawback to it. As he poisons the leaf which will eventually poison the caterpillar, the poisoner also happens to be poisoning himself."

Apparently, Nichols had listened when Rachel Carson sounded the alarm (and started the environmental movement) in 1962 with the publication of *Silent Spring*. Nichols heard her clarion call, rightly claiming *Silent Spring* to be "certainly one of the outstanding books of the twentieth century, or indeed, of any century." While it is the broadscale agricultural application of chemical pesticides that is largely responsible for poisoning the environment, the gardener on his quarter acre must also be held accountable.

Nichols frames the question: "What are we going to do about it . . . we, the average gardeners, going about our small plots, dealing death in our modest little doses?" Ruefully, after narrating the nonchemical alternatives he employs in one experimental season—extract of pyrethrum (an organic insecticide made from this plant's dried flowers), releasing a beetle on the top of an anthill in the lawn, continually hosing the lavender bushes beloved by froghoppers, handpicking and burning the leaves of insect-infected shrubs, gouging out maggots burrowing in the new growth of Scotch firs, removing one by one the slugs eviscerating the hearts of hostas—Nichols concedes that "little, by little we have been obliged to revert to the poisons, with their miraculous but sinister potency. True, we try to use them with discrimination; and we can always console ourselves with the thought that 'everybody's doing it' and that the toxicity of the world at large cannot be greatly affected, one way or another, by the condition of an acre of earth in the county of Surrey." This, he knows, however, to be a specious rationalization, "a barren sort of consolation, for my acre must be multiplied by millions of acres in the charge of other gardeners. And to these acres must be added the tens of millions of acres over which the governments of the world are spreading their daily fumes of death." As Nichols goes back to the chemical arsenal in his tool shed, he leaves the reader with his unresolved conundrum. We hope the world at large is listening to Carson's quiet, scientifically authoritative voice on humanity's heedless damage to Nature's fragile ecological web. But we also sympathize with Nichols as he bows out of the debate; it is sometimes simply too difficult for the gardener to leave paradise until, like Adam, he is expelled.

Spouses in the Garden

EVER since the first couple found trouble in paradise, spousal gardening has been a problematic affair. As we have seen, German Elizabeth's Man of Wrath would have none of it and scolded her for her hours spent outdoors, proving that gardening is for the most part a matter of predisposition. By and large making a garden is best done as a solo enterprise or in concert with a sympathetic mentor or professional guide. However, marriage is fundamentally a collaboration. When one gardening partner is good at one thing and the other at another, that collaboration can sometimes provide spectacular results. What it boils down to is a matter of harmonizing tastes and talents in a way that results in a coherent whole. Sometimes, however, partnership in the garden can be such an entirely mutual endeavor that neither partner can think of any part of the enterprise as "mine" or "yours." In these cases, the garden is something more than merely proprietary and truly deserves the pronoun "ours."

Vita Sackville-West & Harold Nicolson

A peripheral member of the Bloomsbury group, the poet and writer Vita Sackville-West (1892–1962) was an English aristocrat with a Romantic sensibility and deep-seated love of place—in this case her native Kentish landscape and, more particularly, Knole, her ancient, ancestral home from which she was exiled by the law of primogeniture. In 1915, following her marriage to the diplomat Sir Harold Nicolson (1886–1968), the couple established themselves in nearby Long Barn, where Vita created her first garden. The architect Edwin Lutyens was called in to give it form and structure, and the parterre he designed became her learning laboratory.

In 1930 Vita and Harold and their two sons moved to Sissinghurst Castle near Cranbrook in Kent. Here they created the now-famous garden that is today protected as part of the British patrimony by the National Trust. According to their son Nigel in his book *Portrait of a Marriage* (1973), the garden was at the heart of their enduring bond, even as each of his bisexual parents pursued their extramarital affairs. Assuming the role that Lutyens had played at Long Barn, Harold gave the garden its architectural "bones," a series of hedge-enclosed "rooms," and Vita its color and texture. His was the garden's classical component, hers the romantic, a successful aesthetic fusion that other inspired garden-makers of the period, notably Lawrence Johnston at Hidcote Manor, also mastered.

The White Garden, Sissinghurst.

The Sunset Garden, Sissinghurst.

From 1947 to 1961, looking down on the garden from her study in one of the castle's two towers, Vita wrote a weekly column for the *The Observer* called "In Your Garden." Gathered into a series of volumes—*In Your Garden* (1951), *In Your Garden Again* (1953), *More For Your Garden* (1955), *Even More for Your Garden* (1958)—the columns were where she shared with her readers the ideas, practical suggestions, and effects she achieved by certain plant choices and compositional arrangements.

Although in a strict sense an amateur gardener, Vita had a depth of plant knowledge rivaling Jane Loudon's and an artist's eye akin to Gertrude Jekyll's. Thus we see in the development of the garden at Sissinghurst how she complemented her husband's sense of form with her own inspired brand of horticulture. The *Observer* columns take us into that development in real time when the garden is taking shape through experiment and serendipity. Then we see it continually changing as fresh ideas and chance come into play. Their immediacy is engaging, and even from this distance we can enjoy Vita's "this-is-what-I-have-on-my-mind-this-week" writer's stance. Hers is an epistolary approach, for she writes the column in the manner of a letter, which in many cases it is, since her readers were apparently her faithful correspondents. In some cases, we find her briskly dispensing tips:

> A word of practical advice: put a ring of slug bait round each clump [of bulbs] as soon as the pale noses appear, and be quick about it, because the pale nose of to-day is the full flower of to-morrow. Otherwise you will wonder how anyone could ever recommend a thing of such rags and tatters.

Then sometimes she chucks a tart little tirade at her reader:

> I notice that people become enraged over the names of
> plants, and I don't wonder. I wish only that they would not
> blame it on me. 'Why,' they write indignantly, 'why can't
> you give us a good honest English name instead of all this
> Latin?' Well, whenever there is an English name, I do give it;
> I prefer it myself; I would much rather call a thing Bouncing
> Bet than *Saponaria officinalis*; but when there is no name in the
> vernacular, our common speech, what am I to do?

And for anyone who has visited the renowned White Garden
at Sissinghurst, there is a frisson of delight when coming upon
Vita's inspiration for it in her column dated January 22, 1950:

> It is amusing to make one-colour gardens. They need not nec-
> essarily be large, and they need not necessarily be enclosed,
> though the enclosure of a dark hedge is, of course, ideal. . . .
>
> For my own part, I am trying to make a grey, green, and
> white garden. This is an experiment which I ardently hope
> may be successful, though I doubt it. One's best ideas sel-
> dom play up to one's expectations, especially in gardening,
> where everything looks so well on paper and in the cata-
> logues, but fails so lamentably in fulfillment after you have
> tucked your plants into the soil. Still one hopes.
>
> My grey, green and white garden will have the advan-
> tages of a high yew hedge behind it, a wall along one side, a
> strip of box edging along another side. It is, in fact, nothing
> more than a fairly large bed, which has now been divided
> into halves by a short path of grey flagstones terminating
> in a rough wooden seat. When you sit on this seat, you will
> be turning your back to the yew hedge, and from there I
> hope you will survey a low sea of grey clumps of foliage,

pierced here and there with tall white flowers. I visualize the white trumpets of dozens of Regale lilies, grown
three years ago from seed, coming up through the grey of
southernwood and Artemisia and cotton-lavender, with
grey-and-white edging plants such as *Dianthus Mrs. Sinkins*
and the silvery mats of *Stachys Lanata*, more familiar and
so much nicer under its English names of Rabbits' Ears or
Saviour's Flannel. There will be white peonies, and white
irises with their grey leaves . . . at least, I hope there will be
all these things. I don't want to boast in advance about my
grey, green, and white garden. It may be a terrible failure.
I wanted only to suggest that such experiments are worth
trying, and that you can adapt them to your own taste and
your own opportunities.

All the same, I cannot help hoping that the great ghostly
barn-owl will sweep silently across a pale garden, next summer, in the twilight—the pale garden that I am now planting, under the first flakes of snow.

Significant for the time, Vita employed two women as her
gardeners. Graduates of Waterperry, Sibylle Kreutzberger
and Pamela Schwerdt came to Sissinghurst three years before Vita's death in 1962. Like other great gardens that have
become too expensive for upkeep by their owners, Sissinghurst was given over to the National Trust shortly thereafter.
However, even as its paths were stabilized and the garden
made accessible to the general public, because of Kreutzberger's and Schwerdt's training with Vita and their more than
thirty years of subsequent management, followed by that of
Alexis Datta, the current head gardener trained by them, it
has retained the quality of Vita's artistry. The lesson here is

that to perpetuate a garden in the spirit of its creator (one can never perpetuate it as a static artifact), successor gardeners must have not only sound horticultural skills but an innate creativity compatible with that of the original garden-maker. In the most literal sense, this constitutes respect for "the genius of the place."

Margery Fish & Walter Fish

*I*n 1937 Margery Fish (1892–1969) and her husband, Walter Fish, bought a fifteenth-century manor house in East Lambrook, Somerset. Like Vita Sackville-West and Harold Nicolson at Sissinghurst, they created a garden on the land around their ancient abode. But unlike the partnership of Harold and Vita, which was a fusion of two complementary sensibilities, the Fishes' represented a decided clash. Walter Fish adopted the role of boss, which he was in fact when he was the editor of the *Daily Mail* and she was employed as his assistant. In her delightful book *We Made a Garden* (1956) it becomes clear that in those prefeminist days he treated Margery as a minion at home as well as in the office. It is equally clear, however, that the "we" of the title is in fact "she," a deeply knowledgeable and passionate gardener who counters his regimental approach with quiet subversiveness. The undercurrent of tension between husband and wife is subdued, or at least it appears so, since her delightful narrative is devoid of rancor.

How Margery Fish overmastered her husband's authoritarian dictates and achieved a remarkable garden indebted to the English cottage style that Gertrude Jekyll had demonstrated and propounded so influentially, is best told in her own words:

> In addition to roses and clematis Walter had a deep passion for dahlias, the bigger and brighter and the fleshier the better.
>
> He bought a large collection from an expert almost as soon as we bought the house, and the first summer they enjoyed a secluded season in front of the hedge that separated us from the next house. There was no other place then in which to grow them, and I thought it was an admirable permanent home for them, a position all to themselves with a hedge as background, but Walter felt they were being slighted by being put in the background and when I came to plant my terraced garden I was told to leave plenty of large spaces for the dahlias. . . .
>
> Unfortunately they were never labeled, so I had no idea what colours they were. Walter said they were all so lovely that it didn't matter. I held other views but was not clever enough to evolve a way of labeling them. I did try but in the process of lifting the tubers, washing the tubers, drying the tubers, dusting with sulphur the tubers and finally burying the tubers in boxes of ashes the chance of any label remaining attached to the tubers was very remote. The consequence was that I got great blobs of the wrong colour in my carefully planned schemes, which did not endear them to me. They were the most flashy collection of dahlias I have seen, only fit for a circus, as I often told my husband.
>
> When we first started gardening I was only allowed to watch (for future reference) the great ritual of planting dahlias. I think I was permitted to get barrowloads of manure and cans of water, but he would not trust me to do more. In after years, when he could not do the heavy jobs, I had to plant them but he always stood by to see I didn't cheat.
>
> Stock Exchange holidays—the 1st of May and the 1st of

"A General View of the Author's Garden." *We Made a Garden* by Margery Fish, 1956.

November—were our aim for the ceremonies of planting and lifting the dahlias.

First of all Walter dug a large deep hole. He never worried about treading on my plants, or smothering them with the great piles of earth that were thrown up, so I had to be careful not to plant anything within a wide radius. . . .

A little 'fancy' soil (I mean for this good compost or a nice potting mixture) was sifted in all round the tuber and then some, but not all, of the earth dug out was put back. Instead of a nice smooth finish there had to be saucer like hollows to catch the moisture that would come from heaven or the watering can. It was no good for me to tell him that it looked as if the cat had been busy, it didn't matter what my bed

143

looked like so long as each dahlia was given all the comfort humanly possible. When he had finished I used to go round removing surplus earth that was heaped up all round each planting, but I never dared shovel it back into his hollows, as I wanted to do. Some things were sacred.

Watering the dahlias was one of the things I was supposed to do and often shirked. If ever Walter saw me with a can in my hand, giving refreshment to some little stranger, or preparatory to sowing seeds, I knew I should hear 'Are you going to water the dahlias.' I am afraid I got in the habit of doing my watering when he wasn't about. I wouldn't have minded if a small amount of water would have sufficed. Nothing less than a whole canful had to be poured slowly down each horrible little hole—and the contents of one can would bring new life to quite a lot of my small treasures.

Sometimes even the stoutest stake would prove a broken reed and casualties brought gloom into the house. Nowadays, thank goodness, one seldom sees those tall fleshy dahlias, with blooms like heavy soup plates, so heavy they can hardly hold up their heads. I am glad that the present taste is for less tall, less exuberant dahlias, which are easier to grow and far easier to incorporate into an ordinary garden with pleasant effect.

The problem has been solved for me because I was never very successful in keeping tubers through the winter. Unlike the cottagers, whose favorite place for storing them is in the spare bedroom, I have only outhouses and they are all cold and draughty places. Under the staging of a greenhouse is a good place, but I have no greenhouse, and however carefully I stored them, tucking them up in mountains of straw, the cold always managed to find them and every season there were a few less, until I was reduced to two very ordinary red ones, a double and a single, and these I leave in the ground. They come up year after year and I am quite glad to see them.

Following the favorable reception of *We Made a Garden*, Fish went on to become an established and popular garden writer with *An All the Year Garden* (1958), *Cottage Garden Flowers* (1961), and other books still in print today. When we think of her contribution to the field, we need to remind ourselves of the gradual reduction that had gone on in garden size since the great, aristocratic, landowning days when Elizabeth von Arnim made her German garden. For her to indulge herself in the pleasure of gardening was an insult to her head gardener. Such was not the case in the 1930s when both the Sissinghurst and East Lambrook Manor gardens took shape. Within the much smaller house and garden dimensions that had become the norm, gardening was very much an owner-engaged operation. There were helpers to be sure and occasional labor to build walls or perform other kinds of heavy work, but there was no longer any question of there being a head gardener with whom to quarrel. Margery Fish and Vita Sackville-West were their own head gardeners. With (in the case of Vita) and without (in Margery's instance) the support of their husbands, their great accomplishment as garden writers was to make the English cottage-garden style a design paradigm for gardeners whose properties were only somewhat larger than those of the cottagers of old.

Sir Roy Strong & Julia Trevelyan Oman

A noted author of books on gardens and British social history and art, the former museum director Sir Roy Strong (b. 1935) did not come to the garden like Jekyll, Thaxter, Nichols, and other gardeners we meet in these pages with the eager curiosity of childhood. Instead, he was a late and enthusiastic convert. In *Garden Party* (2000) he explains how in the early 1970s he began to tutor himself by visiting all the great gardens of England and Europe. He found that his taste gravitated toward the formality of Tudor gardens and those of the period of William and Mary, and he was seduced as well by the geometries of Italian Renaissance and European seventeenth-century gardens:

> From the outset it was [the] earlier periods which excited my imagination. I stood enraptured at the vast clipped yews at Packwood House, Warwickshire, which depicted the Sermon on the Mount; or wondered at the trim canals and espaliered fruit trees at Westbury Court, Gloucestershire; gazed in admiration at the great borders along the terraces of Powys Castle, in Montgomeryshire, with their lead shepherds and shepherdesses gesturing toward the hills of Wales. Knot and parterre, statue and gateway, maze and pleached avenue cast their spell, one intensified by a passion for Italy. So the discovery of the great Italian gardens fired me in all their crumbling glory, and from them my interest fanned outwards to embrace the baroque gardens of northern Europe.

In 1971 Strong married Julia Trevelyan Oman (1930–2003), an eminent British television, theater, and film designer, who brought a dramatic sensibility and historical orientation similar to his to the design of the Laskett, their three-acre Herefordshire gardens. Begun in 1974, soon after Strong became director of the Victoria and Albert Museum, the couple drew up a design that he says, "emerged out of what I loved and knew best. There was never any question but that the garden was to be formal." The gardens that initially inspired the design of Laskett were all pre-eighteenth-century English ones. However, Strong admits, "The trouble is that, almost twenty years on, so many other influences have come tumbling in. Italy certainly. . . . The Villa Lante and the Villa Farnese haunted me. . . . Het Loo in Holland constantly seized my imagination during the 1980s, with the result that more box and ground pattern began to spring up everywhere."

In addition, Strong conceives of the Laskett as "the portrait of a marriage, the family we never had or wanted, a unique mnemonic landscape peopled with the ghosts of nearly everyone we have loved, both living and dead." In this sense, it is an autobiographical garden, a display cabinet for such career trophies as a stone plaque by Simon Verity "in which my profile is sandwiched between that of the Queen and Prince Consort" (a farewell tribute by the Associates of the Victoria and Albert Museum when he stepped down from its directorship in 1987), as well as personal mementos, notably an urn and other artifacts recalling his wife's distinguished ancestry and a sundial from the garden of his close friend, the portrait photographer Cecil Beaton. Since Oman's death in 2003, parts of the garden, such as the arbor honoring Sir Frederick Ashton, the choreographer for whom she designed two ballets, can be read as recollections of her presence, elements within Strong's idea of landscape as memory and garden as an album of personal souvenirs.

Although as garden-makers Strong and Oman are sometimes likened to Harold Nicolson and Vita Sackville-West, Laskett and Sissinghurst are quite different. An eclectic composition with Tudor and Stuart influences combined with recollections of Italian and Dutch gardens, Laskett's emphasis is on ornamental focal points and garden centerpieces, as well as topiary, knot gardens, and parterres. On the other hand, Sissinghurst's clipped hedges are simply the design framework for a tapestry of ingeniously woven plant shapes and colors. Illustrating the contrast, at Laskett the allée of pleached lime (linden) trees is presided over by a crowned column that commemorates both Queen Elizabeth I and Queen Elizabeth II; the lime walk at Sissinghurst is simply part of the garden's form-giving structure—green architecture for its own sake.

Joe Eck & Wayne Winterrowd

For over thirty years Joe Eck (b. 1945) and Wayne Winterrowd (1941–2010) were partners in the garden as well as in life. The pleasures and rewards of deeply shared mutual interests and talents are evident in their extraordinary Vermont garden and the books that grew from it. They represent that rarity, the dual author who writes with a single voice in which one writer's tone is indistinguishable from the other;

to surmise as to who wrote what passages is futile. There is great merit in such collaboration under circumstances where it is possible, for individual writers benefit from sympathetic critics, and having one so close to hand is a valuable literary asset. In this case, we can guess that Eck and Winterrowd's limpid prose is the product of a good deal of handing manuscripts back and forth.

The two men wrote other books and articles under their individual names, but it is in their first and last jointly written books, *A Year at North Hill: Four Seasons in a Vermont Garden* (1995) and *Our Life in Gardens* (2009), where they convey most intimately their deeply shared joy in nurturing plants and gardening in each other's company. In the preface to the latter, they write, "When two lives have been bent for so many years on one central enterprise—in this case, gardening—there really is no such thing as separately. That is not to say that we do not divide up chores and tasks. Much like piano duetists, we both have our separate parts to play, though we are also concerned that the source of our lives be one seamless and complete whole."

As may be assumed from the title, *A Year at North Hill* is organized, like several other books we are examining here, according to the calendar. Climate, moreover, is implicit in the garden's name, North Hill, and indeed climate runs like a thematic note through all of the Eck-Winterrowd duo's writing, for Vermont—classified as Zone 4 on the USDA map found in most American gardening encyclopedias—presents horticultural challenges not encountered in the higher-numbered

Autumn at North Hill Garden.

plant-hardiness zones further south. Thus if April is not the cruelest month, in northern New England, where the frost goes down three feet, it certainly is the muddiest:

> The earth's unlocking begins at the surface and proceeds by inches downward. Rains and sodden, quick-melting snows fall in the night and sometimes all day long but the hard mass of ice beneath the few inches of just-thawed soil prevents the penetration of the moisture. Mud is the result. It is sometimes so deep that parts of the garden are completely inaccessible, and people who live on more-traveled dirt roads get home only by trusting their fate to the unchurned "back way."
>
> There is a kind of ontological fitness to the mud's preceding the greening of the earth, for both ancient myth and modern science concur that mud—sodden clay—is the mother of life and its first home. And mess though it certainly is—in the garden, in the house, on one's boots, and on the feet of the dog and cats (who *will* go in and out all day long, just like folks, to check on the arrival of spring)—the mud is still exciting, a cause for celebration. And it is not just domestic life

that celebrates: in the warm, moist twilight the red-winged blackbirds signal their return with sweet piercing notes in the highest bare branches, and later in the night the chorus of spring peepers, tiny invisible frogs, reaches a cacophony pleasantly troubling to sleep. From the arrival of that sound until the end of autumn, the true gardener will sleep neither as deeply nor as long as in winter, and will be glad of it.

This "true gardener" is, as we have seen, someone who goes to to great lengths to nurture and protect various seedlings and shoots newly emerged from the soil each spring. The true gardener also takes immense pains to protect already established plants that are loved for their rarity, sheer beauty, and venerable age. We are never in doubt that Eck and Winterrowd fit this description of the true gardener. And since their game is gardening against climatic odds, we learn about the number of tons of evergreen branches they spread over their planting beds for protection, their heavy labor muscling numerous weighty oversize terracotta pots containing warm-weather plants onto a back porch or into a spare bedroom that they keep heated to around fifty degrees in the winter, and how diligently they have worked on various parts of the property to build windbreaks and provide other forms of cold-climate protection for their plants. These things are the outgrowth of deep place-based knowledge, understanding of the workings of nature in various ecological situations, persistent effort, and success through trial and error. Thus, they have been able to match each plant's growing requirements with the most hospitable ecological niches available, some of which they have created themselves. They maintain, "For the true gardener, the pleasure of finding just the spot where a plant wants to grow is always greater than growing it in just the spot the gardener wants. Success then becomes a partnership rather than a bully-ing (and often a futile one) of the plant by the gardener."

Not surprisingly, through their considered alliance with nature Eck and Winterrowd greatly enlarged the number of species they were able to grow at North Hill. Compare their ingenuity in this regard with the carefreeness of those who garden in Britain's more forgiving climate. Blessed by the mitigating effects of the Gulf Stream and reliable rainfall, English gardeners take their mild winters for granted. They rarely mention the kind of stratagems the Vermont pair had to resort to in order to have a broad array of plants thrive in their garden. But gardening challenges are, in fact, what Eck and Winterrowd delight in. Running throughout their books is a plethora of interesting information on how to cos-set plants normally too tender to grow this far north. Mag-nolias, for instance, are definitely an out-of-Zone-4 plant and an early flowering tree we associate with southern gardens. Winterrowd, who grew up in Shreveport, Louisiana, loved them since childhood, as did the Pennsylvania-born Eck. For-tunately, their favorite Massachusetts nursery stocked one variety, *Magnolis x loebneri* 'Merrill', the only semihardy speci-men that far north. Naturally, back in 1970s when they began to make their North Hill garden near Readsboro, they bought one. With no little pride, in *Our Life in Gardens* they report their success in growing it: "This first tree now stands more than thirty feet tall, with three elephantine trunks ascending from

the ground, each dividing into muscular branches that termi-
nate in a mass of twigs. All winter long their tips are decorated
with fat, fuzzy gray buds that hold the promise of spring, seem-
ing ready to split their calyxes in any warm spell."

But could they be satisfied with one magnolia? Winterrowd and Eck confess that they are collectors by nature. Plant
collectors are especially ardent in their pursuit of difficult-to-
obtain varieties; they were thus eager to assemble as many
different species in their garden as possible. Remarkably,
there are now thirty-eight different kinds of magnolias at
North Hill, the result of mail orders from such faraway places
as Gossler Farms Nursery in Springfield, Oregon, from which
they were able to acquire a *Magnolia stellata*, one of the two
parents of the 'Merrill', the other being *M. kobus*.

In this way they became fascinated with plant genetics,
and as their collectors' passion prompted further acquisitions,
they began to hunt for varieties of the same plant, the result
of crossbreeding species of different parentage within a particular genus. Thus, when they were able to track down a *M.
x soulangeana* 'Alexandrina', they planted one by their stream
and discovered to their delight "that if any tree can accept
percolating water near its roots, it gains at least a zone in hardiness." This success story concludes with the happy report
that this tree "has never failed to bloom, even after our cold-
est winters." Other triumphs follow. When they found out
that *M. virginiana* would also tolerate water-logged soil they
planted six in boggy places along the stream. By the 1980s,
plant breeders had engendered a number of other species

"The bank along the side of the barn is clothed by a very hardy English ivy, *Hedera helix* 'Baltica'. The annual Himalayan impatiens, *Impatiens glandulifera*—a glamorous plant that grows to eight feet and is full of flowers throughout July and August—self-seeds into the bank. Roughly 3 percent of those that come up may be allowed to stay, the rest laboriously weeded out. But they are worth the trouble."

– From *A Year at North Hill: Four Seasons in a Vermont Garden* by Joe Eck and Wayne Winterrowd, 1995.

"January begins the camellia show, and the first is a curious Japanese form in the higo class called 'Yamamato Nishiki'. It is a single one, with a thick boss of yellow stamens and unpredictable carmine variegation across its white petals."

– From *A Year at North Hill: Four Seasons in a Vermont Garden* by Joe Eck and Wayne Winterrowd, 1995.

whose hardiness descended from *M. acuminata*, which, when crossed with more tender species, introduced the color gold to the magnolia genus. Starting with the largest-flowered one, 'Elizabeth', which was brought into general cultivation by the Brooklyn Botanic Garden in 1977, the abundance of new varieties rapidly multiplied. But out of this happy event another problem arose, and this called for more strategic thinking: "When gardeners are confronted with a plethora of new plants in a genus they adore, the only possibility is to contrive some special place for them. That prevents the garden from becoming jittery because forms of a favorite plant are scattered all over the place." Grouping plants led them to create a magnolia walk on either side of the pergola. It leads through the woods to the guest house, the daffodil meadow, and beyond the meadow to the vegetable garden—incidentally, the subject of a third literary collaboration, *Living Seasonally: The Kitchen Garden and the Table at North Hill* (1999).

With more species available, the collectors found they could double or quadruple their magnolia choices. They selected 'Butterflies', 'Ivory Chalice', 'Miss Honeybee', and 'Yellow Lantern'. Soon a magnolia orgy was underway, and they were planting "four specimens of *M. x* 'Who Knows What', called that because they are seedlings gathered from our garden, and are of indeterminate parentage. Two have pure white flowers and one is the palest pink, indicating to us that 'Merrill' and 'Leonard Messel' had gotten together at some point."

In addition to becoming expert plantsmen in their own right, Eck and Winterrowd learned a great deal from the garden writers who went before them. It is not surprising, therefore, to find scattered throughout their books references to Vita Sackville-West, Margery Fish, and Reginald Farrer, to name just three. We imagine Farrer's nod of approval as we read the caption for an illustration in *A Year at North Hill:*

> Having been assured that many cranky alpines would thrive in coarse, gravelly sand, we filled our planted wall with 'bank run.' *Daphne cneorum* var. pygmaea thrives on such a lean diet, bearing its richly fragrant flowers at nose level on top of the wall. An even greater feat than growing a finicky alpine plant was the creation of the rock garden itself, a piece of serendipity of the kind that delights the true gardener's soul.

And we are reminded of one of Jane Loudon's beautiful illustrations in *The Ladies' Flower-Garden* when we read:

> High above the planted walls at the other end of the garden, among the roses and peonies, opium poppies are in flower by late June. These are known botanically as *Papaver somniferum* from their use since ancient times as a soporific. But their rich, bosomy opulence makes them most unlike their California and Mexican cousins. They are sometimes called "lettuce poppies," or even "bread-seed poppies," for that is the most benign of their uses. They are in fact the source of opium, and of its refined forms, morphine and heroine, but here, they are grown for the beauty of the flowers.

In the alphabetically organized *Our Life in Gardens*, a series of charming mini-essays on subjects ranging from *Agapanthus*—lily of the Nile—to the almost-impossible-to-obtain southern-Australian *Xanthorrhoea quadrangulata,* they summon the ghost of Margery Fish, whose opinion they quote under "H" for "Hellebores." According to her, Hellebores should be grown as separate clumps, so that each plant makes a picture with its flowers and leaves . . . I like to come across my hellebores in odd places."

They steeped themselves in information gleaned from the old herbals of Dioscorides, Gerard, and Parkinson:

> *Helleborus niger*, the earliest to bloom, is called the Christmas rose, and *H. orientalis*, flowering a month or so later, the Lenten rose. Parkinson first made the comparison in the seventeenth century ("like unto a single rose"), and it fits, if one thinks of the wild, five-petaled English eglantine.

No doubt, Eck and Winterrowd are as annoyed by slugs as any of the other gardeners we encounter in this compendium, but as we move from "Hellebores" to "Ilex," we find they have a surprising pest in mind when they take offense at the robin. Understandably they are cheered in the snowy Vermont winter by the bright red berries on the three tree-size bushes of *Ilex verticillata* growing almost to the height of the cedar-shingled roof of their gray-clapboard house. This is why they complain:

> We are hardly alone in our appreciation [of *Ilex verticillata*]. For though we have few guests at this season, the garden is not unvisited. In early October, just before the weather gets crisp and the leaves turn, robins begin their flight south, and our garden lies squarely in their path. To us, it is a mystery that the robins prefer the three ilex across the front of our house to those growing in the wild, with berries so numerous on the twigs that they weigh the branches to the ground.

We see such bushes all along the highway from the Canadian border well into southern New Jersey and beyond, and they are never robined. Perhaps house-grown berries are tastier, or perhaps the prevalence of well-stocked bird feeders has made the birds believe that the best things are often to be found around people's houses. Or maybe they are just eager to make us miserable, intruders, after all, in a world they knew long before us.

The philosophy implicit in this last sentence is one worth pondering. Stoically, like Beatrix Farrand who oversaw the dismantling of her Reef Point garden in Maine, they have looked with sober realism at the sure fate of theirs:

It is a curious thing to "own" land, as in "This is our own land; we own it." For we are, after all, only the briefest moments in its existence, even though we have worked it as a garden on its surface and inhabited its space for our best time on Earth. Its history is traceable before us, in the memories of our oldest neighbors, and in town records and deeds. We know that the Carpenters and Spragues owned it before us, and there is frequent testimony to their presence in bits of household detritus—glaucous, mud-filled medicine bottles, shards of slate gray pottery, a rusted horseshoe that caused one of them to curse, having lost it, a century ago. When such things are turned up by our shovels, or by the feet of the cows, we muse on them, and on their lesson, as we go about our work. . . . Now we, too, have added our subtle accretions to the land, first by making a garden on it, and then by writing a book about it. It will not easily shake off either imposition, though certainly the words we have written about it will go first. But for how many centuries might there be the subtle tracery of a stone wall or path, the abundant progeny of *Impatiens glandulifera*, even naturalized stands of *Meconopsis betonicifolia?* We do not find any of these ideas terrible, even if there is no one, no gardener as we understand the word, to wonder and admire. But the thought does give us a shiver. That much we will admit.

Others speak of the ephemerality of gardens, of how quickly they are reclaimed by ordinary nature once they are abandoned. Today there are many fine gardens in which this lament has been countered with strategies for preservation. The British National Trust and the Garden Conservancy in the United States are admirable in their efforts to perpetuate the lives of certain fine gardens. But Winterrowd and Eck's inclination to accept the dissolution of theirs stems from the realization that, even though they have had a professional practice as garden designers, *gardening*, rather than the *garden*—the verb, not the noun—has always been the point. True gardeners to the end, they would never want to declare North Hill "finished." Now, keeping in mind Winterrowd's recent death not long after the legislature of Vermont made possible his and Eck's formal marriage, we can read the last words of *Our Life in Gardens* as both a parable about gardening and a testimony to the joys of enduring love.

> When we were both in our twenties, on a lovely spring morning we decided to fly a kite. We bought a kit, with balsam ribs and tissue paper and string, and we spent the whole morning assembling it. It was a very fine kite, crimson red and deep blue, and we put it together pretty well, given the fact that we had no particular experience in the construction

of anything except chicken cages, at which we thought what we had done was a good job. The Public Garden across from which we lived had no free space for running up a kite, so we crossed Charles Street, and launched our kite by running up the hill of Boston Common. It went splendidly, and soon it became a speck in the sky. But the allowance of string in the kit was meager, and so one of us ran back down Charles Street to buy another spool. When we tried to tie one end to another, the wind was strong and the kite slipped free. We watched as long as it was visible, and when we could no longer see it, we went home.

This event occurred at the very beginning of our gardening life and our life together. It seems to be a paradigm of our experience here. And we ask anyone who should visit in years to come to remember that gardens always depend on the constant care and the vigilance of their creators. After that, they are shadows. Or a speck in the sky, as our kite became.

Correspondents in the Garden

E MUST PAUSE here for a moment to wonder what will be the effect in terms of archival longevity as well as the tenor and tone of garden writing in the new information age. What happens when email has replaced pen-and-ink correspondence and there are no actual letters in libraries? In terms of the writer's voice, is the Internet's capability of reaching a much larger audience through social networking and blogging a fair trade-off for a more intimate form of communication? It seems fair to assume that letter writing, whether to a personal friend or the presumed ones garden columnists address as fellow gardeners, strikes a more candid note than a Facebook posting.

For now, however, we can be glad that among the letters exchanged by garden writers over the epistolary centuries, some have found their way into books such as the ones we are discussing here. As their authors bring you through their metaphorical garden gates and invite you to stroll with them in your imagination, they tell you many interesting things and offer a good deal of sound advice based on experience. Their manner is one of casual information sharing—blooming times, nursery-catalogue critiques, planting tips, and so forth. Almost universally, they convey the impression that gardeners are perhaps the happiest—if sometimes most frustrated—of mortals.

Garden columnists, disciplined by a recurring deadline and short word count, seem to find this style of writing particularly congenial literary form. Even though their column is not an actual letter to a fellow gardener, it often sounds like one. Not surprisingly, many of their readers do write them back, thus making them assume the burdens (and pleasures) of a personal correspondence.

Jean-Jacques Rousseau

*W*e think of Jean-Jacques Rousseau (1712–1778) as Romanticism's apostle, the exponent of nature as humanity's benign nurse and best teacher. The great Enlightenment *philosophe* did more than simply prescribe a new kind of education isolated from the falsities of society; he also produced a botanical curriculum based on his mastery of the *Species Plantarum*, the 1753 publication whereby Carl von Linné (better known Carolus Linnaeus) revolutionized the science of botany by introducing a universal system of nomenclature. Intended as a means of popularizing the new Linnaean system, Rousseau's *Lettres sur la botanique* employed the literary conceit of presenting what is in effect a primer in the form of a series of letters written to Madame Madeleine-Catherine Delessert between 1771 and 1777, in fulfillment of her request for a method to teach her young daughter the principles of botany. As in his novel *Émile*, the letters, with their advocacy of an instructional method based on observation rather than rote learning, Rousseau was promoting his revolutionary and then-controversial philosophy of education.

Impressed with Rousseau's accessible pedagogy, which he adopted in his own teaching, Thomas Martyn (1735–1825), Regius Professor of Botany at Cambridge, translated the collected letters along with Rousseau's introduction, which he published in English in 1785 under the title *Letters on the Elements of Botany, Addressed to a Lady*. Martyn dedicates his translation "To The Ladies of Great Britain No Less Eminent for their elegant and useful accomplishments than admired for the beauty of their persons."

In his introduction, Rousseau takes pains to explain the confusion caused by the prevalence of multiple systems for naming plants and the scientific boon conferred by Linnaeus in classifying plants according to their genus and species, thereby providing "the advantage of a new language, which is as convenient and necessary for Botanists, as that of algebra is for mathematicians." The basis for the Linnaean system is the subdivision of genera into various plant groups based on their sexual characteristics rather than their appearance—that is, the construction and number of their pistils and stamens. Championing this method of botanical classification, Rousseau asks "every reader of common sense, how it is possible to attach one's self to the study of plants, and at the same time to reject that of nomenclature."

However, one must not begin merely with the naming of plants. He therefore tells Madame Delessert in the first letter, dated August 22, 1771:

You desire to have a little catalogue of the most common plants [but] I find some difficulty in doing this for you . . . without using language peculiar to the subject. . . . Besides, merely to be acquainted with plants by sight, and to know only their names, cannot but be too insipid a study for a genius like yours; and it may be presumed that your daughter would not be long amused with it. . . . We have nothing therefore to do yet with the nomenclature, which is but the knowledge of a Herbalist.

Thus floral construction is his primary lesson, for fructification—the fruiting of the plant—depends on this. After defining and explaining such terms as corolla, pistil, stigma, stamen, filament, anther, and calyx, he assures Madame Delessert that his educational philosophy is the proper approach to instructing her child. Investigative discovery of "the mysteries of vegetation . . . will unveil to her by degrees no more than suitable to her age and sex."

Beginning with the lily family, he continues in subsequent letters to outline other plant categories: cruciform (cross-shaped), pea (leguminous), labiate (two-lobed), umbellate (springing from a common center), compound (multifloret), and so forth.

In Letter VIII, dated April 11, 1773, he explains how to make a herbarium, and the following March he assures his correspondent:

I have received your packets very safe, and cannot but admire the neatness with which you have taken in having all the parts necessary to determine the genus and species in your specimens; and the brilliancy of colour in most of the flowers. All this serves to show how much better the female fingers are adapted to such operations than ours. I am pleased to hear that our little Botanist had so large a share in laying out and drying these plants, which I shall carefully preserve as a memorial of the industry and adroitness of both. But what gives me the most pleasure is, to see that you have remarked, with so much success in general, to which of the natural classes your plants belong: so that I am convinced you have profited by my lessons, and have paid due attention to my letters.

On March 25, 1774, in Letter IX, he says with good reason, "Do not suffer yourself to be terrified at the word system," as at last he gets down to the technical distinctions that constitute the basis for Linnaean taxonomy. But now it is no longer Rousseau who is speaking but rather Professor Martyn, for although the sixteen letters following the original eight are purportedly by Rousseau, they have reached a level of instruction more appropriate to the candidate for a Ph.D. in botany than the mother of the would-be "little Botanist." Martyn has simply chosen to continue Rousseau's epistolary format in setting forth the distinctions between different plant families, the names of which are based on the number of stamens each genus within it possesses: *monandria* (one), *diandria* (two), and so forth on up to *decandria* (10) and *didynamia* (from 11 to 19). But since these "letters" are really only textbook chapters, it is here that we take leave of Rousseau and his impersonator in the hope that the fair ladies of Great Britain were able to stay the course.

Thomas Jefferson

As *Thomas Jefferson's Garden Book*—an annotated compilation of garden diary entries and letters to botanists, nurserymen, and fellow gardeners—makes abundantly clear, President Jefferson (1743–1826) was America's first great garden writer. For Jefferson, natural history embraced the uncultivated lands as well as the agricultural fields of Monticello and beyond, where the flora and fauna of a vast continental wilderness awaited classification. As president, he commissioned the Corps of Discovery in 1803, thereby sending Meriwether Lewis and William Clark on the first overland journey to the Pacific Coast and back. On his return, Lewis was able to bring descriptions of a hundred seventy-eight hitherto unknown species as well as the seeds of numerous wild plants, a triumph in the infancy of botanical science and a source of lively transatlantic plant exchange. It was an exciting period: the botanical exploration accompanying colonial expansion was bringing plants from faraway lands into cultivation in English and Continental botanical gardens, most notably the Royal Botanic Gardens at Kew in southwest London and the Jardin des Plantes in Paris. These exotica were as eagerly sought in America as its own native plants were abroad.

Between 1785 and 1789, when he served as minister to France, Jefferson was as diligent in learning about native European species and recent foreign plant introductions as he was about studying architecture—his other lifetime passion. He formed a lasting friendship at that time with André Thouin, the premier botanist in France, and this set in motion a transatlantic exchange of seeds and plants that continued over the course of many years. Thus he was able to obtain numerous species not native to America, which he planted at Monticello and shared with David Hosack, founder of the Elgin Botanical Garden in New York City, and Bernard McMahon, the Philadelphia nurseryman who propagated and grew numerous plants from abroad. At the same time, McMahon maintained that American gardeners should not be so enamored of foreign plants that they "neglect the profusion of beauties so bountifully bestowed upon us by the hand of nature." Many of the plants he grew were from seeds Jefferson had received from the Lewis and Clark expedition. His *American Gardener's Calendar* (1806), the young country's most authoritative and comprehensive gardening manual, served as Jefferson's horticultural bible. Jefferson's own botanical garden was, of course, Monticello, and here he took great delight in growing an array of trees and shrubs, their seeds coming from both the American wilds and Europe.

While Jefferson was facilitating the introduction of foreign plants into his country, European aristocrats were setting aside portions of their estates as American gardens. When he was residing in France, several of his French friends asked him to obtain plants for them from American sources, the most notable of which was John Bartram, Jr., whose botanical garden and arboretum on the banks of the Schuylkill River was then the center of a large seed trade.

The Comtesse de Noailles de Tessé, whose salon he frequented, became a particular friend of Jefferson's, and after he visited her château de Chaville outside Paris, the two began a regular correspondence that continued until her death in 1813. In the years following his return to America, she sent him the seeds of various exotic species, and in 1811 he was pleased to report to her that the native Chinese golden rain tree (*Koelreuteria paniculata*), the first of its kind in the United States, was flourishing at Monticello.

After she was forced to leave Chaville, he encouraged her with these words:

> I learn with great pleasure the success of your new gardens at Auenay. No occupation can be more delightful or useful. They will have the merit of inducing you to forget those of Chaville. With the botanical riches which you mention to have been derived to England from New Holland, we are as yet unacquainted. Lewis's journey across our continent to the Pacific has added a number of new plants to our former stock. Some of them are curious, some ornamental, some useful, and some may by culture be made acceptable to our tables. I have growing, which I destine for you, a very handsome little shrub of the size of a currant bush. Its beauty consists in a great produce of berries of the size of currants, and literally as white as snow, which remain on the bush through the winter, after its leaves have fallen, and make it an object as singular as it is beautiful. We call it the snow-berry bush, no botanical name being yet given to it, but I do not know why we might not call it Chionicoccos, or Kallicoccos. All Lewis's plants are growing in the garden of Mr. McMahon, a gardener of Philadelphia, to whom I consigned them, and from whom I shall have great pleasure, when peace is restored, in ordering for you any of these or of our other indigenous plants.

To furnish the new garden at her Auenay estate, she and Jefferson continued their seed exchange. She was obviously a knowledgeable and discriminating collector of American plants and was continually sending him itemized lists of seeds she particularly wished for him to procure for her. Fulfilling these requests was not easy. Writing from the White House on January, 30, 1803, he lamented that he could send her "those articles only which the fruits of this neighborhood, or its gardens can furnish"—*Liriodendron tulipifera* (tulip tree), *Juglans nigra* (Eastern black walnut), *Juniperus virginiana* (Eastern red cedar), *Sassafras albidum* (sassafras), *Magnolia glauca* (white magnolia), *Magnolia tripetala* (umbrella magnolia), *Cornus florida* (flowering dogwood), *Catalpa* (Indian Bean Tree). To obtain these, he "engaged an old Scotch gardener of the neighborhood, who had formerly lived some years with my family, to undertake this collection." Shifting into a more intimate vein, he expressed concern for her poor health at present and shared with her his dream for the days he would spend at Monticello in retirement:

> I own, my dear madame, that I cannot but admire your courage in undertaking now to plant trees. It has always been my passion; insomuch that I rarely ever planted a flower in my life. But when I return to Monticello, which may be in 1805, but will be in 1809 at the latest (because then, at any rate, I am determined to draw the curtain between the political world and myself), I believe I shall become a florist. The labours of the year, in that line, are repaid within the year, and death, which will be at my door, shall find me unembarrassed in long lived undertakings.

We get a glimpse of the length of time and the difficulty of transatlantic plant transport when we find Jefferson nine months later informing Madame de Tessé that the plants listed above were finally going to be shipped. Apologizing for the lateness of the departure of the 13-cubic-foot box of seeds, Jefferson instructed:

> By casting your eye on a map you will perceive that to send a package from [Washington] to Baltimore, Philadelphia, or New York to be reshipped to France, is as difficult as to send one from Havre to Marseilles for America. . . . It remains therefore that we depend solely on Alexandria, which has not a great intercourse with France. It happens fortunately at the moment that we are sending a ship on public account to the Mediterranean, but to touch on Lorient [on the coast of Brittany] on her way.

He then explained that this container of seeds would be addressed to the U.S. consul at Lorient, and that she could advise him of the best method of sending it on to her, adding that if it were not too late he would try to see if seeds of the live oak and catalpa could still be found, since these were on her original list and the ship hadn't yet left dock.

Further confirming the problems involved in transatlantic transportation, in March 1805 we find Jefferson apologizing to Madame de Tessé because shipment of the collection of seeds he had had assembled for her that year had been rendered impossible by icebound harbors on his side of the Atlantic and on hers by the blockade of Le Havre caused by the Napoleonic wars. (Le Havre was at the time the only viable port in terms of the cost of commercial shipping). This meant that "we are therefore completely defeated for this year in the new supply of plants; & must comfort ourselves with better hope for the next."

The difficulties with regard to seed transportation did not abate, nor did Jefferson and Madame de Tessé's efforts to exchange plants. Just before her death, he wrote that he "was mortified not long since by receiving a letter from a merchant in Bordeaux, apologizing for having suffered a box of plants addressed by me to you, to get accidentally covered in his warehouse by other objects, and to remain three years undiscovered, when every thing in it was found to be rotten."

But gardening is a future-oriented enterprise, and completing a garden is never a realistic goal, or perhaps not even a desirable one, for no real gardener would want to make a garden that was not continually growing and changing in spite of unforeseen mishaps and his or her own mistakes.

Katharine S. White

An engaging prose style sets the fine garden writer apart from the mere garden journalist. Katharine S. White (1892–1977), a longtime editor at *The New Yorker*, was such a writer. In addition, she was a discerning critic of the styles of other writers, including the authors of garden catalogues, a subgenre of gardening literature that she highlighted in fourteen articles she wrote under the subhead "Onward and Upward in the Garden" for the Books section of the magazine. Married to fellow *New Yorker* staff member E. B. White, she gardened on a small farm in Maine. Leaving New York

City for a year-round life in the country was not her idea, but it was here that her husband was happiest, writing and raising animals (a source of inspiration, it may be imagined, for his classic children's book *Charlotte's Web*) while she conducted her editorial responsibilities long-distance. White gardened with unflagging passion and continued to write her inimitable garden-ing essays for *The New Yorker* in spite of several bouts of debilitating illness. Fortu-

Katharine S. White, *Onward and Upward in the Garden,* 1979.

nately for us, following her death in 1977, E. B. White collected them in a single volume, and *Onward and Upward in the Garden* (1979) has taken its rightful place as a classic among the genre of books we are examining here.

White's brand of informal limpidity was of its period, one that I would characterize as "Old New Yorker": urbanely quirky, humorously serious, and leisurely in pace. Under the magazine's founder, Harold Ross, she was instrumental in shaping its tone and style. It is a voice that remains unique in the annals of journalistic prose and one that William Shawn, the magazine's subsequent editor, perpetuated for the next thirty-five years.

Combining her editor's sensibility with her inspiration to turn her avocation of passionate amateur gardener into print, White laid claim to a new department of literary criticism in her first "Onward and Upward" piece, dated March 1, 1958:

> For gardeners, this is the season of lists and callow hopeful-ness; hundreds of thousands of bewitched readers are poring over their catalogues, making lists for their seed and plant or-ders, and dreaming their dreams. It is the season, too, when the amateur gardener like myself marvels or grumbles at the achievements of the hybridizers and frets over the idiosyn-crasies of the editors and writers who get up the catalogues. They are as individualistic—these editors and writers—as any Faulkner or Hemingway, and they can be just as frus-trating or rewarding. They have an audience equal to the most popular novelist's, and a handful of them are stylists of some note. Even the catalogues with which no one man can be associated seem to have personalities of their own.

Digging into her subject, she was able to surmise that "the sage of White Flower Farm, in Litchfield, Connecticut, who signs his writings 'Amos Pettingill' " was using a pseudonym for effect (she later learned that his real name was William Harris, one obviously devoid of colonial Yankee flavor). What she really appreciated about this individual were the nursery bulletins called *White Flower Farm Notes:* "Here Amos really lets himself go, is chatty, sassy, or lyrical, as the mood dictates, and here he airs his latest enthusiasms and his pet grouches."

White was addicted to the catalogues, and her list of seedsmen and nurserymen at the back of *Onward and Upward in the Garden* is helpfully keyed to the pages where you can reread what she has to say about each of them. Glancing at my copy now, I see many check marks indicating that I must have ordered several of these catalogues when I was a neophyte gardener. Besides this bibliography of catalogues, E. B. White has helpfully provided another one composed of all the books to which she referred in these collected essays. It contains numerous titles, several of which we are already familiar with, since her library of literature on gardening was extensive. It is not surprising while reading White, therefore, to renew our acquaintance with Jane Loudon, Gertrude Jekyll, William Robinson, Louise Beebe Wilder, and Elizabeth von Arnim.

Garden writers in the pre-Internet age often established extensive letter-writing networks, querying one another, sharing information, and giving practical advice. Their communications were, needless to say, more interpersonal than the postings of the modern blogger. In those days nurserymen answered customers' letters, frequently offering news about their families along with fiercely idiosyncratic opinions. In White's case, she corresponded with several such nurserymen and liberally quotes from their letters to her. But her richest and most rewarding exchange was with her fellow gardener and garden writer, Elizabeth Lawrence.

A fan letter from Elizabeth to Katharine shortly after the first "Onward and Upward" article appeared in *The New Yorker* initiated a rich epistolary friendship that lasted until the latter's death. Although the two women, one writing from Maine, the other from North Carolina, only met face-to-face once, the successes and failures they experienced in their respective gardens, the mutual esteem in which each held the other, and the sympathetic concern they felt for one another as their later responsibilities and afflictions took them beyond the bounds of garden talk, give their letters a life of their own. Fortunately, Emily Herring Wilson has preserved one hundred sixty-six of them in *Two Gardeners: Katharine S. White and Elizabeth Lawrence: A Friendship in Letters* (2002), a valuable selection exemplifying the fact that garden writers are a community—a social network, or if you prefer an older terminology, "brothers and sisters of the spade."

Elizabeth Lawrence

Elizabeth Lawrence (1904–1985), was born in Marietta, Georgia, attended Barnard College, and then returned to live in Raleigh, North Carolina, with her mother, who was an avid gardener. There she designed gardens for friends, became a contributor to *House & Garden* magazine, and published her first book, *A Southern Garden* (1942). In 1948 she and her mother sold their large, impractical house and legendary garden in Raleigh and moved to Charlotte, where they lived next door to Elizabeth's sister Ann and her family. Here, on a smaller scale, Lawrence created another garden, and it served as the primary inspiration for her writing thereafter. As her confidence grew, she became a noted authority on gardening in general and gardening in the South in particular. In 1957

she was asked to contribute a weekly column to the Charlotte *Observer*, and like Vita Sackville-West, she found this
format perfectly suited to her relaxed, conversational style.
She made her column, in effect, a hub of correspondence, a
means of sharing the wealth of horticultural information she
received from other gardeners who wrote her—and they
were numerous, indeed.

Happily, other garden writers have taken on the job of
building her reputation as one of the foremost authors in this
genre. In his preface, Allen Lacy explains how he "conjured"
Gardening for Love: The Market Bulletins (1987), a book she had
long intended to write, from a mass of Lawrence's papers left
for safekeeping in a pasteboard box at Duke University Press.
Its subject, the market bulletins in which Southern farmers
used to advertise agricultural products and animals for sale and
their wives the seeds of native plants they grew in their gardens,
stemmed from her correspondence with these women and her
reports in the *Observer* on the plant lore she learned from them.
Bill Neal, her friend of many years, took on the job that E. B.
White performed for Katharine White, compiling according
to the months of the year a selection of her *Observer* columns,
which he published under the title *Through the Garden Gate*
(1990). Lawrence's biographer, Emily Herring Wilson, continued the task of burnishing her well-deserved reputation with
the publication of *Two Gardeners: Katharine S. White and Elizabeth
Lawrence: A Friendship in Letters* (2002) and *Becoming Elizabeth
Lawrence: Discovered Letters of a Southern Gardener* (2010), drawn
from her voluminous correspondence with friends and relatives.

In her garden columns Lawrence often mentioned such predecessors as German Elizabeth, Jane Loudon, Gertrude Jekyll, and Vita Sackville-West. It is not surprising, therefore, to find one dated January 25, 1959, devoted to Jane Loudon. Lawrence begins by saying that she had recently been delighted to receive a volume of essays on nineteenth-century gardeners that described Loudon's books and garden in Bayswater. According to her report of what she had just read, a picture of this garden emerges. She maintains, moreover, that *Gardening for Ladies* could still be consulted as a reliable source of horticultural information a century after it was written.

> The garden in Bayswater was small, only a quarter of an acre, but two thousand species, and no telling how many varieties, of trees, shrubs, vines, roses and herbaceous plants grew within its walls. The lawn was so thickly planted with several hundred sorts of bulbs that the grass could never be cut. There was also a hothouse for tropical plants, and an alpine house with six hundred pots. There was even a collection of mosses. . . . Mrs. Loudon had material at hand for any number of garden books, and having found that there were none for the amateur, she set out to write them for the Victorian ladies who were beginning to take an active interest in gardening. . . . Since Bayswater, a suburb of London, has winters very like ours, Mrs. Loudon's books have a particular interest for gardeners in these parts.

Lawrence was prone to draw on the words of Homer, Shakespeare, Pope, and other canonical writers, as, for instance, when she begins her column of August 30, 1959, with "The hum of bees is the voice of the garden, a sound that

Elizabeth Lawrence
in her garden.

lends new meaning to the flowers and the silence; music that
has not changed since Virgil heard it and wrote of Heaven's
gift, honey from the skies." She also counted as old friends
Jane Austen, Willa Cather, and other novelists.

On July 7, 1968, reflecting on nocturnal scents, she told
her readers that "Mrs. Price, who knows how I like perfume
after dark, gave me a pot of the night-scented geranium
(*Pelargonium gibbosum*)." This sent her to her bookshelf to
find her favorite books on sweet-smelling plants, where "one
of the most pleasant is Mrs. Gaskell's story of *My Lady Lud-
low*." She continues, "My lady divided scents into two classes, the delicate and the vulgar, and when a young man came
to church with a spring of lads-love (as the cottagers called

southernwood) in his pocket, 'she was afraid that he liked coarse pleasures.' " This, in turn, directed her thoughts to Gertrude Jekyll in whose book *The Scents of the Garden* she found "many more distinctions than the mere difference between the delicate and the vulgar." With keen olfactory discrimination, Jekyll had opined that sweet scents—roses, honeysuckle, primrose, cowslip, mignonette, pink, carnation, heliotrope, lily of the valley—are "wholly delightful." Continuing to quote, Lawrence conveys Jekyll's opinion that "there is a class of scent that is intensely powerful and gives an impression almost of intemperance or voluptuousness, such as magnolia, tuberose, gardenia, stephanotis and jasmine." She adds, "Miss Jekyll took the greatest pleasure in aromatic leaves. When crushing a bay leaf, brushing against rosemary or treading on thyme, she felt 'that here is all that is best and purest and most refined in the range of the faculty of the sense of smell.' "

There are circles within circles, and in another column Lawrence calls on her predecessors Jane Loudon and Louise Beebe Wilder to advise Katharine White on the properties of the gas plant (*Dictamnus albus*). Summoning Loudon as her initial authority, she says that what she calls "a phosphoric vapor" from this fragrant flower is reputed to be easily ignited by a candle. Lawrence herself, however, had never beheld this wonder, an emission of bluish flame. Nor had "Mrs. Wilder [who] says in *The Fragrant Path* that repeated experiments on her part 'failed of any spectacular results.' " Appending her own comment, Lawrence reports, "my own gas-plants (planted hopefully every fall for a number of years) never survived long enough for the evenings to be hot and still. So I am just as eager as Mrs. White for hers to light up, and I think Maine is a good place for it."

In what has by now become a familiar theme among our group of garden writers, Lawrence was prone to evoke the scenes of childhood. Her *Observer* column of August 9, 1959, pays tribute to family members and flowers in the same breath:

> Some time ago my cousin Harriet sent me a lavender stick from Greece. She wrote that she had bought it from a laven-der-woman on the streets of Athens because it reminded her of Grandmama. Every summer, Grandmama used to weave sweet-scented sticks for us from the lavender that grew in the little garden outside of her parlor window. I wish I could remember what else grew in her garden. I do remember old roses; little pink lilies that we called sand lilies, and that I later found to be *Zephyranthes grandiflora*; and a bush of lemon-verbe-na which would live through the winter in Marietta, Georgia.

Lawrence was a defender of the author of *Silent Spring* when Rachel Carson's polemic was still considered controversial, but her own conservation perspective remained local. Although the depredations of various creatures such as squirrels, moles, woodchucks, and birds might prod other gardeners into active warfare against them, Lawrence was all empathy, taking the side of her garden residents in the battle of humankind and na-ture. On January 6, 1963, she told her readers:

> I find it hard to live anywhere without slipping into the role of murderer. Last spring I sent Ulysses up on a ladder to clear out the nest that the sparrows had built under the eaves. He cleared them out, baby birds and all. And yet the young of

the sparrows must be as dear to them as young wrens are to wrens.

I had supposed that as I grew older I would become hardened to the suffering of small animals, but I find that as my gardening fingers thicken, my skin grows thinner than ever. And even at moments when the garden seems to be happy, a shadow falls, and there comes to mind an echo from childhood:

> He hears the cry of the little kit fox,
> And the lemming in the snow.

A garden catalogue maven like Katharine White, Lawrence tells us in the beginning of *Gardening for Love* how pleased she was when "years ago Eudora Welty told me about the old ladies who sell flowers through the mail and advertise in the *Mississippi Market Bulletin*, published twice a month by the Mississippi Department of Agriculture." She was enamored with the "sweet country names" she found in this and other market bulletins put out by state agricultural departments in the South, all of which she subscribed to (this practice did not occur in the North to her knowledge).

Lawrence's seed and bulb orders from the farm women who advertised in these publications predictably initiated a new stream of correspondence. By ordering seeds from them, she entered into their network of plant and information exchange. Much of this correspondence focused on nomenclature. For example, Mrs. Grady Stamps, of Bogue Chitto, Louisiana, told her that the moon lily she advertised in the *Mississippi Market Bulletin* as "night glow" was called that in the *Louisiana Market Bulletin*, the source of her plant seed. The correspondence with Mrs. Stamps extended over several years as seeds began to be shipped in both directions:

> Mrs. Stamps said she would be glad to have seed of any-
> thing I have that is new—meaning new to her—so I looked
> around the garden to see what was going to seed and found
> fennel and *Clematis texensis*. Mrs. Stamps wrote me right back:
> "I never did have the fennel, and the clematis seed you sent
> are larger than any I have seen. . . . I love to work with
> flowers, advertise, and get letters from people. . . . As long
> as I can, I'll work with my flowers, but I am about to get
> [too] disabled to work much in them like I used to, so I want
> bulbs and perennials that will stay there. I must stop now,
> or I won't have room to enclose some seed. I love to give as
> well as receive."

After going back and forth with Mrs. Stamps about the
plant she called devil's pincushion, Lawrence satisfied her botanical curiosity by sending a stalk Mrs. Stamps had sent her
to "Dr. Solymosy, who identified it as *Leonotis nepetifolia*, a native of tropical Africa which has been naturalized in the South
from Tennessee and North Carolina to Florida and Louisiana."
When she informed Mrs. Stamps of this, the answer came back,
"They always have another name than the one we go by. . . .
Wish I knew how to get those botanical names to all flowers."

The letters between "Miss Lawrence" and "Mrs. Stamps"
about this and that species continued. As in her letters with
White, over the years a more personal relationship emerged
and family matters mingled with garden talk. In January 1975
Lawrence received a letter in which Mrs. Stamps explained a
long silence by telling her that she had been sick for two years
and had recently lost her husband. Gardens always grow in the

shadow of mortality, and their histories become the reflections of old age. Summing up what had given her life pleasure, Mrs. Stamps said, "I just love flowers and wherever I go if I find anything different I beg or swap. That's how I got started selling seeds and plants through the market bulletin. . . . When I had more plants than I needed I thought it would be interesting to sell. And it is! It makes mail time more fun and gives me a little extra change."

Of all Lawrence's many correspondents, the one she valued most was Carl Krippendorf, a retired Cincinnati businessman whose one hundred and seventy-five acre estate east of Cincinnati, called Lob's Wood, was blanketed with innumerable small bulbs—scillas, *Chionodoxa*, *Eranthis*, *Galanthus* (snowdrops), *Leucojum* (snowflakes), and many species of daffodils, which he had "colonized by the millions." Since they lived in different horticultural zones, many of their letters, which began in 1943 and continued until his death in 1964, consisted of reports on different varieties of bulbs and their respective blooming times in Ohio and North Carolina. Lawrence's *The Little Bulbs: A Tale of Two Gardens* (1957) is dedicated to "Carl with Love," although within the text she never refers to him as other than Mr. Krippendorf. Her preface begins:

> This is a tale of two gardens: mine and Mr. Krippendorf's. Mine is a small city back yard laid out in flower beds and gravel walks, with a scrap of pine woods in the background; Mr. Krippendorf's is hundreds of acres of virgin forest. Both are perfect for little bulbs, for no garden is too small to

hold them all if only a few of each are used, and no forest is too large to show them off if enough of one kind is planted. While I content myself with a single daffodil, Mr. Krippendorf likes to see ten thousand at a glance. Where I plant half a dozen, he plants a hundred.

Because of the depth of knowledge of so many bulb varieties she and Mr. Krippendorf share, her writing here verges on the technical. As in her garden columns, in *The Little Bulbs* she positions herself as the moderator of a conversation with previous authorities, contemporary friends, and Mr. Krippendorf. In one of the letters included in the book she quotes Mr. Krippendorf's reply to her inquiry about the blooming times of snowdrops. His answer was:

> With me the Byzantine snowdrop is the earliest, blooming before Christmas. It has much wider leaves than *Galanthus elwesi*, which blooms in open weather in January. *G. nivalis* is the English snowdrop, with grasslike foliage. Usually it blooms in February or early March. . . . Have you ever noticed the delightful scent that snowdrops have?

At this point Lawrence chimes in, saying that Mrs. Wilder had noticed the same and then proceeds to quote her as follows:

> Earliest come the snowdrops, pale children of the snows, that carry within their frosted bells the first faint fragrance of the year. In sheltered places in my own garden they bloom early in February if not buried beneath heavy snow, and I have more than once known them to take advantage of an amazing interlude of mild weather in January to slip out of the half-frozen muck and flower serenely.

She adds, "In Charlotte, I have found the Byzantine snow-drop in Mrs. Church's garden early in November, and when the weather is not too bad it blooms on through Christmas and into spring. Hers is an old planting in the light shade of deciduous trees on a western slope."

After the death of Carl Krippendorf and his wife Mary, Lob's Wood was put under the protection of the Cincin-nati Nature Center and renamed Rowe Woods after Stanley Rowe, Sr., who, along with twelve other environmentalists, founded the center in order to protect the Krippendorf lega-cy. In 1966 Lawrence visited Lob's Wood, and at the behest of the Nature Center, she produced a small book describing the sanctuary. Drawing on their twenty-three years of corre-spondence, she was able to conjure up in minutest detail the appearance and blooming times of Mr. Krippendorf's incom-parable collection of bulbs. Thus, Lawrence can say with un-disputed authority that at Lob's Wood, "tulips began with the magnificent Red Emperor. Mr. Krippendorf spread one of the flowers out, and found that it was nearly twelve inches across—almost vulgar, he said. The brilliant flowers of Ad-vance, a very early scarlet May-flowering tulip, came two weeks later; and at the peak of the season, the long, lily-like pure white flowers of White Triumphator, and the blazing Parade." Sounding a bit like Celia Thaxter or Louise Beebe Wilder, she goes on to describe this last according to her own enthralled observation: "The enormous flower of Parade is scarlet with a rosy glow. Its black stamens and yellow stigma, and the many-pointed star in the center, outlined by a pale yellow halo, make a gay Persian pattern that reminds me of the tulip's provenance."

Because of their long and close friendship in letters, Carl Krippendorf continues to live in Lawrence's pages along with the beauty of his flowers. Such is Lawrence's legacy: the ability through words to keep flowers blooming in many gardens—Mrs. Stamps's, Mr. Krippendorf's, and, of course, her own.

Gene Bush

I recently received my 2011 catalogue from the Munchkin Nursery & Gardens, a family-owned business located in Depauw, Indiana. Taking note of the down-to-earth descriptions of this year's offerings of native and nonnative shade perennials, Munchkin's specialty, I thought how refreshingly old-fashioned: a catalogue just like the ones that used to delight Katharine White and Elizabeth Lawrence! My hunch was that this one had come in the mail from a nursery that only publishes on paper. Googling to check, I realized that my forebodings about the future of garden writing were probably out of tune with reality. I had assumed that the intimate tone of catalogue writers that Lawrence and White cite met its inevitable demise with the arrival of the Internet, but the website of Munchkin's proprietor, Gene Bush (pause and take note of how frequently some surnames correspond with professional identities!), proves that even online an idiosyncratic and personal style of garden writing still flourishes.

I learned on the Munchkin home page that Bush is a married man and that his wife JoAn is his business partner and fellow gardener. He could thus have been placed in either of two categories we have already considered: "Spouses in the Garden" or "Nurserymen in the Garden." But the friendly and personal tone of Bush's monthly blog posts seem to me to align him more appropriately with the garden writers we call "Correspondents."

Gardening came late in life for Bush. Once aroused, his gardening zeal equalled that of Carl Krippendorf's, and his property began to reflect his passion. After taking up residence in southern Indiana, he started with vegetables but soon moved on to flowering plants. This switch in focus came literally by accident when the tractor with which he was cutting grass nearly went over a small cliff, causing him to realize that planting the hillside with trees and shrubs would relieve him of the danger of steep-terrain mowing. Soon he was a nursery catalogue addict. Fifteen years later, he claims, "The garden now fills the hillside, spilling over to fill almost every niche of my life. It is my place of peace and serenity as well as my hobby."

His explanation of why he christened his garden "Munchkin" has a fairy-tale quality and could only have been written by someone who is perennially young at heart:

> The question most often asked is Why the name Munchkin?"
>
> At 6'2" I am a bit tall for a Munchkin.
>
> Much of my childhood was spent playing in the woods alone or with buddies. The forest has always held a special fascination for me.
>
> A sense of the mysterious hiding behind each tree, along with the quiet one could feel, appealed to my young imagination. A sense of intimacy from being embraced and

surrounded by all the tall trees always felt comfortable.

One special place of peace and security always existed for me in the woods as a child. I remember a brook tracing the base of a small hill, rippling around smoothly worn stones. Halfway up the hill was a rock ledge reached only by climbing a sharp incline. Behind the ledge lay a gently curved pocket of cool emerald green moss. Many afternoons were spent laying there feeling the cool green on my back with warmth on my face watching the clouds wander through my imagination and across the sky.

It has been over 40 years since I visited my secret place in reality, but I have always carried it in my heart and mind.

No surprise that when I moved to Indiana my home would have woods on the 5 acres and I would have a woodland garden. A garden on the side of a hill centered around a small rock cliff framing a wet weather spring.

Munchkins are mythical little people who live a childlike existence in the wood. They are also noted for being funloving and mischievous. Perhaps they became my alter-ego. In any case, what better moniker for one who loves the forest, woodland plants, and has a nursery specializing in woodland and dwarf wildflowers than the name *Munchkin.*

The Munchkin shade gardens are located on the north side of a rolling hill in southern Indiana where the slightly acidic soil is heavy clay over limestone. Bush describes how they began coming to life in the early 1980s as he amended the soil and created raised beds to accommodate plants with special needs. He explains that although he is essentially a plant collector, he tries not to let the overall garden design appear as a series of collections. He achieves this effect by first planting native species and then letting curiosity serve as his guide. If there are nonnative relatives of indigenous species, he allows them to immigrate into the garden. He characterizes this merger of the local and exotic as an "exuberant wild garden."

Being shade-loving plants, various species of native ferns are Munchkin specialties. Bush believes that "there is a fern for every niche from groundcover to major feature." In one posting of his blog, he focuses on the walking fern, *Camptosorus rhizophyllus:*

> My idea was to duplicate nature and have the ferns mature, touch their frond tips to the moss and form colonies of ferns up on the rocks. I transplanted to amended soil and gravel next to the rocks and was astounded by their rapid growth the first two years; when what I had expected was a struggle. By the 3rd year fronds were touching the mulch and the moss-covered rocks, forming tiny duplicates of themselves. . . . A friend gave me an old log with a split down its middle and that now has old potting medium with starts of moss filling the cavities and transplants of walking fern nestled inside. I will probably transplant more starts over the cave entrance in the center of my garden.

Another blog posting is about seed collecting:

> Plants disperse their seed in almost as many ways as there are flower families. Hardy geraniums have tiny built-in catapults that literally throw seed when it is ripe.
>
> Trilliums and violets have fleshy "tails" on each seed that ants can not resist and the seeds are carried away to be buried in tunnels. Butterfly weed has silken parachutes to drift away on the wind.

Now for a novel tip:

> My preferred method to catching seed before it disperses
> is with pantyhose or nylon knee-highs.
>
> Since I was a bachelor for some years this method was
> quite time-consuming and expensive. Not the collection of
> the seed, for that was easy, but the obtaining of the panty-
> hose was the most difficult part. . . .
>
> Plants do not seem to be particular as to pantyhose style.
> Sandal toe or nude is equally fine. Sheers allow light and air
> to still reach the seeds. Nylon does not hold moisture so the
> seeds will not mildew. Cut a length of hose to fit the size of
> the stem holding the seedpods. The first cut to form a tube
> begins above the toe end upward to desired length. After the
> toe cut, tie off one open end of each new length with thread,
> forming another tube. I like to use brightly colored thread to
> keep the catchers visible. . . .
>
> Slip the stocking tube over the flowers after they have
> been pollinated and are beginning to form pods.
>
> Tie off with more thread below the blooms, gently wrap-
> ping the stocking around the stem so fine seed cannot escape. . . .

It might seem that we are hearing an echo of Čapek's farcical
offer of the clothes off his back to his struggling plants in the
dead of winter when he adds:

> Visitors to my garden often inquire about why I have stock-
> ings on my plants. My usual reply is the older plants need
> support hose from standing on their roots all day.

Lawrence's correspondent Mrs. Stamps would have been
especially happy to have had the Munchkin catalogue arrive
in her mail, for it contains a helpful table that pairs common
plant names with their Latin equivalents. You will find the

same thing online, but you might want to order a paper cata-logue for handy reference. It is well worth the $4.00 subscrip-tion fee, especially since half the fun is thumbing through a real garden catalogue, circling the plants you plan to order.

Leafing through this year's, I am tempted to order one of Munchkin's new introductions, the 'Misty Blue' variety of *Actaea pachypoda*, a native shade plant commonly known as "doll's eyes." Here is how Bush describes it:

> And is it ever blue! Foliage is very distinctive light bluish-silver over green that truly lights up a shady corner. Same growth habit of 2 to 3 feet in height and spreads to the same width over time with multiple stems. Blooms in spring re-semble white bottle brushes in a dome shape well above the leaves. Pollinated flowers turn to white berries with black dots, or eyes, each one at the end of a reddish pedicel in sum-mer. Twice the bang for your garden buck.

If I had a rock garden I would also think about ordering some yellow stargrass (*Hypoxis hirsuta*), a tiny plant only six inches high with softly hairy blades. It grows from a "small tuber about the size of your little finger nail." I may be wrong, but since it is an American native and not an alpine or Himalayan species, I doubt that Reginald Farrer had this small plant in his Yorkshire garden. Bush placed his yellow stargrass at the base of a dwarf hemlock, among limestone rocks, knowing that there it would seed and form small, open colonies. Well, maybe I could start an e-mail correspondence with Bush and see what he has to suggest about how to create a rocky niche where I can effectively isolate this lime-loving plant from the rather acidic soil of my Long Island garden. . . .

Conversationalists in the Garden

CLOSE cousin to the garden correspondent, the garden conversationalist is the kind of writer who seems to be chatting with you over drinks. Even more so than some of the writers we met earlier, conversationalists are likely to adopt the role of congenial host, delighted visitor, or frank critic. As in a conversation among familiars, the thoughts they share with you are random and personal.

Hugh Johnson

*P*rimarily recognized as an eminent wine expert and the author of numerous, best-selling guides in that field, Hugh Johnson (b. 1939) brings his encyclopedic approach to other plants besides grapes, most recently to the publication of *The World of Trees* (2010). Perhaps as an ongoing diversion from the arduous discipline of writing comprehensive reference works, several of which have to be periodically updated, Johnson has long had a tandem career as a dedicated gardener and garden writer. His "diary," as he calls the column he has written for the past thirty-five years, began when he helped revamp the *Journal of the Royal Horticultural Society*, rechristening it *The Garden*, a title paying homage to the magazine with the same

Saling Hall, Essex

name published by William Robinson a hundred years earlier. From the beginning, he adopted a nom de plume, another act of homage, this time to the early seventeenth-century botanist and royal gardener John Tradescant. Since then Trad's diary (Tradescant now goes informally by the nickname bestowed on him long ago by Johnson and his readers) has migrated from one publication to another and today rests happily within the pages of the quarterly *Hortus*. Fortunately for non-subscribers, Johnson has recently put out *Hugh Johnson in the Garden: The Best Garden Diary of Our Time* (2009), a selection of Trad's previous entries that validate the book's otherwise boastful subtitle.

Johnson's tone is spontaneous and off-handed. Think of a casual e-mail informing you about something that strikes his fancy or piques his curiosity on a given day. However, few e-mails are this interesting to read. Couched in terms of the experiments and experiences this day-to-day gardener is constantly gathering, his words have immediacy—as well as

authority—based on his vast knowledge of plants and horticulture. More profoundly, they convey Johnson's deep sense
of place. In his case, the place is Saling Hall, an ancient manor
dating from the twelfth century, which he and his wife Judy
purchased in 1970. Here, next to the long brick manor house
with a protruding Dutch gable at one end, with the village
chapel visible through the trees, he made a garden. They now
have two other gardens—one in central France and one in
Wales—in which Johnson experiments with different soils,
climates, and ecosystems. Nevertheless, the voice in his column is usually that of Trad writing from his study in Saling
Hall, a genial man pondering his thoughts as he looks out at
the same, but always different, garden he created and has re-
created over the past forty years.

Love of a particular plot of earth—the passion that ani-
mates most good garden writing—plus the ability to create
the kind of word pictures that make illustrations unnecessary
can be sampled in Trad's diary entry for June 2000, which he
titled "Blink and You've Missed It":

> This year blackthorn seems less precocious than everything
> else in the garden, and at Saling has coincided perfectly with
> our massed amelanchiers; mounds, now, of pink-tinged
> white that close-to match the blackthorn in intricacy of a
> million tiny petals. This is my desert-island bush, the amel-
> anchier; the annunciation of spring and the fiery farewell of
> autumn. We planted a score of them 20 years ago and have
> never regretted it.
>
> Brilliant against this background are kerrias, magnolias,
> chaenomeles, flowering currants, mahonias (still), pieris, and

at ground level anemones, violets, scillas, pulmonarias, berge-
nias, daffodils, hyacinths, primroses and wallflowers. Each is
a sharp, shocking independent outbreak of energy from bare
ground or bare twig; nature incoherent with excitement, and
looking on I am panicked by what I am missing in the rush.
'Hold it,' I want to say; 'wait till my senses have registered
everything.' There is time in the other seasons. Not in spring.

And here is the paean to soil offered by Trad in his entry
for July 2004:

> There is a perfect moment for planting in early May, when
> the earth is as full of life as the bundles of roots you are hold-
> ing in your hands, and leaf-green seems to stain the very air.
> Long soaking in the rain and a week of good draining weather
> has made the ground so soft and open that you scarcely need
> a trowel to make a hole, and when I scoop with my hands in
> the fragrant soil to fondle it round the fragile roots I feel my
> fingers would take root too if I left them there any longer.
> Weeds come up as easily as plants go in; there is an almost
> sexual relationship between earth and plant. The ecstasy is
> short-lived, but that is the nature of ecstasy.

The garden at Saling Hall is not without design, but it is
not design qua design, a plan sketched and then implemented.
Rather it is design as a long dialogue with the landscape itself,
one that incorporates Johnson's gleanings from travel as well
as observations and advice from books, friends, and readers.
Design for him is sometimes a matter of happy effect achieved
by intuitive action, as when he cuts a *claire-voie* or peephole in
a hedge, a circular opening that reveals a cameo of what is on
the other side—a statue of Bacchus and a white mulberry tree,

perhaps. Such was the case in June 2002, when Trad told of his delight in having created "Thisbe's Chink," which set him to looking for "the next opportunity to introduce a glimpse of one part of the garden from another, otherwise unrelated."

Eleanor Perényi

*E*leanor Perényi (1918–2009) was a magazine editor and writer as well as the author of a biography of Franz Lizst. Like German Elizabeth, Perényi gave up her American homeland when she married a Hungarian baron in 1937 and went to live on his family estate, where she made a garden in "a large rather mournful park." Though she did not have to endure the displeasure of a disapproving husband, the social mores of provincial central Europe had not changed since Elizabeth's time, and the opinion of the aristocratic set in which she moved was still opposed to the eccentricity of a chatelaine who wished to be a dirt gardener.

Indeed, it was an act of defiance on Perényi's part that she started the garden at all, inasmuch as her husband's baronial estate was located in Ruthenia, "under the brow of the Carpathians with winter winds that seemed to come straight from Siberia." Before her plants could take hold, however, World War II routed her from this harsh paradise (Ruthenia was subsequently made part of the Soviet Union), and her Hungarian garden became only a melancholy memory. *Green Thoughts: A Writer in the Garden* (1981) grew out of her second garden in Connecticut where, transplanted back to her native land after her divorce in 1945, she continued her ardent avocation.

Green Thoughts is a delightfully quirky compendium of randomly dispensed personal experience, historical facts, and acerbic advice. This unconventional garden book uses the alphabet as an organizing principle for an array of disconnected discourses on all manner of things. For instance, a quick look at the table of contents shows under D through F: "Dahlias," "Daylilies," "Earthworms," "Endive," "Evergreens," "Failures," "Fennel," "Frost," and "Fruit," while M takes care of "Magic," "Making Notes," "Mazes," and "Mulches."

Perényi's tone often rises to a polemical pitch. Defiance, as we shall see, continued to define her attitude about horticulture and much else besides. For a sample of her piquant, opinionated prose, look at "Dahlias." Here she huffs:

> Looking at my dahlias one summer day, a friend whose taste runs to the small and impeccable said sadly, 'You do like big, conspicuous flowers, don't you?' She meant vulgar, and I am used to that. It hasn't escaped me that mine is the only Wasp garden in town to contain dahlias, and not the discreet little singles either. Some are Renoir girls; others are like spiky sea creatures, water-lilies, or the spirals in a crystal paperweight; and they do shoot up to prodigious heights. But to me they are sumptuous, not vulgar, and I love their colors, their willingness to bloom until frost kills them and, yes, their assertiveness. I *do* like big flowers when they are also beautiful.

No Margery Fish, she!

From here Perényi goes on to tell us a great deal about the history of the dahlia, a native of Mexico, which was reputedly introduced to European cultivation by the Madrid Botanical Garden in 1798. Not true, she says, taking exception to the date by asserting that the Spanish were importing all sorts of treasures, including floral ones, to their country long before the end of the eighteenth century. She argues that even though they possessively asserted their New World botanical hegemony with a 1566 ban on plant exploration within the empire by non-Spaniards, there was nothing to prevent the dispersal of plants already introduced in Spain to other parts of Europe earlier than 1798. For example, we have reliable information that marigolds, and probably dahlias too, were grown in medieval monastery gardens. Furthermore, it is an established fact that a Swedish botanist, Andreas Dahl, for whom the flower is named, obtained sufficient species of dahlia tubers to crossbreed the plant sixteen years before the Madrid Botanical Garden reclaimed and celebrated Spain's primacy with regard to the introduction of the dahlia.

Perényi then goes off on an educational tangent, comparing the Spanish and English botanical presence in the New World. She says that we must not blame the Spanish for trying to maintain control over botanical discovery in the Americas or for being selfish in repossessing the dahlia as "their" flower. They gave as good as they got—literally. In exchange for corn, tobacco, the potato, the tomato, and other crops and vegetables, "they paid their debt to Amerindian agriculture by introducing wheat, peaches, grapes, olives, figs, lettuce, oranges, pears, barley, onions, and countless other crops to the New World that, in Anglo-Saxon myth, they ravished."

There follows a riff on colonial plant acquisition: "Nothing, after all, is easier than smuggling seeds and bulbs, and where piracy failed, diplomats with their immunity to baggage inspection were most helpful." Thus "in 1750, the German ambassador to Mexico sent flower seed to his botanist friend Gottfried Zinn, for whom the flowers were eventually named." I had never before given a thought to the naming of the zinnia or the dahlia, but I was certainly happy to discover these nuggets of nomenclature in Perényi's essay.

But let's go back and hear her praise Spain some more. The gardens the Spaniards created in several parts of Latin America were sumptuous. English horticulturists weren't a patch on the Spanish, whose "reports from the Indies were more concerned with flowers and fruits than with any other subject, including gold—beginning with Columbus himself, who regretted he hadn't brought a botanist along on the first voyage and thereafter wrote repeatedly of the botanical wonders he saw." Perényi queries with ire, "Why isn't this made clear in the encyclopedias?" She believes it is "because of a built-in bias in most Anglo-Saxon sources against Latins in general and Spaniards in particular . . . [which is why] pirates like Drake and Hawkins are heroes for having stolen plants like the potato from the Spanish colonies, while the very names of the Spaniards who propagated them are unknown."

But we were speaking of dahlias, weren't we, and isn't it time to return to Perényi's Connecticut garden? Here too we can find a connection with Iberia, which will rationalize her previous long excursus and vindicate her contrarian attitude toward those Wasp neighbors who only grow "tasteful" dahlias, if they do not spurn them altogether. Although she does

not divulge its identity, her "New England village" is Ston-
ington, Connecticut, on Long Island Sound, and many of her
neighbors are Portuguese fishermen. Naturally their gardens
are not the type of cottage gardens admired by those she considers snobs—Gertrude Jekyll, Vita Sackville-West, Margery
Fish, and their ilk. In opposition to what she believes is the
preference for pastel-hued flowers of these cottage-garden
proponents, she asserts:

> Our Portuguese fishing families with their grape arbors, their
> vegetables interplanted with tall old roses are in that (alas
> fading) tradition, and dahlias are one of their specialties—
> some of them brought long ago from the Azores to blaze
> like bonfires against the picket fences. I identify with these
> exuberant patches, closer to my heart than any number of
> carefully chosen evergreens and ground covers set in wood
> chips, and won't allow that their owners are less talented
> gardeners. It is my Portuguese neighbor who advises me
> about dahlias, she who tells me to ignore the conventional
> wisdom and plant them early or there will be no flowers be-
> fore August. Plant them deeply (say, ten inches), and they
> can go in well before the last possible frost in May because
> their shoots won't yet be above ground by then.

Passing along what she has learned from the Portuguese
gardening neighbor, Perényi tells us how to divide dahlias
and pack the tubers for storage over the winter (never mind
if the labels fall off, for "the occasional surprise is as likely
to be pleasant as the reverse"). Along with other useful tips
Fish would have ignored in order to diminish the ranks of
these gaudy flowers so admired by her husband, she tells us

how to stake them so that they will be held in their upright positions as much as possible when equinoctial storms would otherwise flatten them to the ground.

Perényi preaches the imperative of good soil and speaks of compost with an almost religious fervor:

> When fully "cooked," it looks like the blackest, richest soil in the world—or a devil's food cake. But it isn't soil at all, and in the earlier stages of decomposition you see, impacted like the layers of an archaeological site, what it is made of. This will vary from garden to garden. In mine, leaves and grass clippings are the chief ingredients—then cabbage stumps, pea vines, hydrangea heads, apples, hedge clippings, spent annuals, carrot tops, and I am sometimes afraid of coming on the fragile skeleton of a bird or mouse, though I never have—all the debris, in short, that the unconverted pay good money to have raked up, bagged, and carried away to the dump or removed by the garbage men. The compost heaps devour them all and returns them in a form that is priceless while costing nothing.

In her entry on "Weeds," as elsewhere, she sides with the organic angels. When she reads in the gardening encyclopedias about "weeds" (note that she puts the word in quotes to indicate irony), she lists several pretty-sounding names of plants that are traditionally classified as such. Her list includes black-eyed Susan, buttercups, white clover, crane's bill geranium, nettles, mallow, St.-John's-wort, celandine, *Veronica officinalis*, tansy, yarrow, sorrel, and many other wild flowers and potherbs. She then fulminates about the appalling assortment of weed killers needed to eliminate them, none of which she would touch after the one and only time she betrayed her commitment to organic gardening. Here is nature's remonstrance for this lapse:

That year's help was flatly opposed to weeding the lawn by hand and I myself was recovering from an operation. I accordingly applied the type of herbicide that is combined with fertilizer, and was promptly punished. Mild though the application was, owing to my qualms, it finished the weeds all right, and grass too; but the worst was yet to come. The following year the weeds returned in redoubled numbers and the grass was in such a terrible state that compost had to be applied like compresses on a wound.

And were he still going about his business in the woods, I would feel sorry for poor chastened Herbert Durand once Perényi had finished giving him a piece of her mind on the sin of digging up wild flowers:

There was a time when we could have looted all this natural beauty without compunction. It had, in fact, to be done, or we would have had no flowers to grow in our gardens, since all are descended from some wild variety that caught somebody's eye. But—it can't be too often emphasized—that time is gone. No longer is it permissible to venture forth with a trowel and a view to improving a naturalistic patch in one's own garden.

Her annotated appendix on catalogues assesses the pluses and minuses of several nurseries with more brutal frankness than Katharine White and Elizabeth Lawrence would have chosen. For instance, here is what she has to say about the Burpee Seed Co.:

One of the oldest and once the best all-round seed house in the country, Burpee in recent years has been trying to be all things to all gardeners and now carries plants ranging from roses to shade trees. You could order a complete garden from their catalogue. The point is, would you want to? . . . The prices of shrubs, fruit trees, berries, etc., compare unfavorably with those of firms specializing in these things and offering more sophisticated choices. . . . I hate to knock Burpee. They were part of my gardening education. But the overpricing and the fact that their seed is no better than anyone else's have turned me away from this respected old firm. On the other hand, February wouldn't be February if their catalogue didn't arrive on schedule.

Robert Dash

*R*obert Dash's (b. 1934) Madoo in Sagaponack on Eastern Long Island is by its creator's reckoning an American garden with an English ancestry. By this, he emphatically does not mean an English-style garden in America. *Notes from Madoo: Making a Garden in the Hamptons* (2000), composed of contributions over a number of years to a column in the *East Hampton Star*, shows a gardener's imagination that places itself with well-read admiration within the tradition of Gertrude Jekyll, Vita Sackville-West, Reginald Farrer, E. A. Bowles, Margery Fish, Hugh Johnson, and other inspired English gardeners, while inflecting this British inheritance to accomplish in American terms a feat similar to theirs: the attunement of garden and place in a way that transcends mere harmony to become something entirely original—a cohesive work of landscape art.

Historically speaking, the South Fork of Long Island is not far behind Jamestown and Plymouth Rock with respect to English arrival in the New World. Its settlers came from the shire of Kent in 1656 to farm the rich, alluvial soil deposited by the last retreating glacier and to graze their cattle on the grassy downs around Montauk. The geological similarity with their native landscape was countered, however, by the contrast of climates. As noted before, the transoceanic transfer of warm Gulf water to the coast of northern Europe by the flow of the Gulf Stream blesses the British Isles with benign temperatures and abundant rainfall, rivaled only by Japan's in terms of gardening ideality. Farmers' fields and gardens on the eastern seaboard of the United States are, if less vulnerable to the harsh extremes of those of this country's continental interior, nonetheless more challenged by drought, heat, and freezing temperatures than English ones. Thus there is no mild, year-round weather with predictable amounts of gentle rain to be counted on. Nor did the original landscape of hardscrabble farmers look the same as that of country squires and rural villagers. The English have the mellow brick of centuries-old manor houses and the rustic picturesqueness of half-timbered, thatch-roofed Tudor cottages as part of their native architectural vocabulary, which several of the gardeners mentioned above have incorporated into the design of their gardens. Americans left a distinctly different mark upon the land, in spite of their British colonial origins, and the visual language of old New England, from which eastern Long Island's first settlers came, consists of wood shingles, white clapboard, and split-rail fences.

These, then, are the parameters within which Dash had to work when he began to make Madoo in 1967: an architectural heritage of weathered wooden barns, good soil of loamy tilth, and a climate designated Zone 7 by the American Horticultural Society, meaning a location in which plants are hardy within an average minimal temperature range of 0°F to 5°F (-10°C to -17.7°C). But these givens are only part of the picture, and "picture" is indeed the right word here, for Dash is an artist, and it is this sensibility as well as horticultural know-how that have guided his every move in the making of Madoo. Thus he can say, "It would need a maul to separate [my garden] from its profoundly English influences. Yet it might take a wedge struck with equal force to pry it from its continuous involvement with the pattern of abstract expressionism, a largely American form of painting." Here is how he describes the other factors that inform Madoo:

> Within that pattern much else went toward the making of my garden: a love of Indian Paths, rather like the secret walks small children make (which counts a lot for how one moves through my garden); an admiration of the roan beauties of abandoned farmland pierced by red cedars laced and tied by dog roses, honeysuckle, and brown, dry grass; the memory of a meadow of a single species of short, gray-leaved, flat-topped, open-flowered goldenrod, whose October display was feathered by hundreds of monarch butterflies. I have a stubborn Calvinist belief in utility, which causes me to plant vegetables among flowers, use herbs as borders and berry bushes as ornamentals. The

brutish littoral climate leads me to choose only such plants as have infinite stamina. There are recollections of an ancestor who planted hollyhocks at the gate and lilacs out back—but all gardens are a form of autobiography. Moreover, as a painter, I am predilected toward shape, mass, and form and have learned that the predominant color of all gardens is green and all the rest is secondary bedeckment. Finally, there is something else—a fierce addiction to privacy, which is why my windbreak is thicker than it need be.

Like Hugh Johnson's garden in Essex, Dash's Long Island garden is forever a work in progress and should be likened perhaps to a palimpsest or a painting with numerous pentimenti. "The successes," he says, "more often than not, are the result of bold throws. I started from the house and went toward the edges, often revising solid achievement until they seemed made of finer matter, like marks and erasures of work on paper, which sometimes may be torn and fitted again in a collage."

The words "toward the edges" are worth repeating, for herein lies a significant difference between American and English gardens. In America, there had not been, as in England, an enclosure movement whereby common lands were transformed into private property, with hedgerows and belts of trees circumscribing estate boundaries. It can be further posited that America's more democratic politics and proclaimed classless society is manifested in an endless suburban landscape in which houses are set within a sea of green lawn. Dash, of course, is anything but suburban in outlook, and we have already heard how much he prizes the privacy of enclosure. But within the garden itself he advocates a unified openness of design:

> To my way of seeing, a garden is not a succession of small
> rooms or little effects but one large tableau, whose elements
> are inextricably linked to the accomplishment of the entire
> garden, just as in painting all passages conduce to the effect
> of the whole. Lack of keyed strength in any one of them may
> lower the pitch and thrust of the finished canvas.

In other words, much as Dash admires Jekyll-descended
English gardens with their linked but discrete pictorial elements set within shrub- or wall-defined garden spaces, he
seeks greater scenic continuity. Thinking of his garden plot
as an unframed canvas, he has one section blend casually with
another and the whole merge to the extent possible with the
surrounding rural landscape.

The only problem here is that this rural landscape of open
fields running to meet the dunes is being replaced by mega-
mansions whose "landscaping" does not in the least fit with
Dash's ideal of a garden set within a frame of farms. Sagaponack,
though still in the Township of Southampton, is now considered one of the socially chic Hamptons (even the subtitle of his
book, "Making a Garden in the Hamptons," concedes as much).
Almost immediately after he bought the two barns that became
his alternating winter and summer studio and living quarters,
the proximity of his property to the pristine eastern stretch of
beautiful Atlantic beaches, with their amber-rose-white sand
running the length of Long Island's southern shore, his rural surroundings began a new life as real estate for the rich. Potato farm-
ing, the mainstay of the local economy since the early years of
the twentieth century, started its inexorable decline. In a chapter he calls "The Death of a Field," Dash expresses his dismay:

In the open fields of Sagaponack, spring is the first brown throw of earth falling over rye cover as a tractor cuts broadly, Sagg Main Street to Sagg Pond and then, engine regeared, pond back to street. Directly to the south this is, in Foster's fields, the widening brown finally meeting a horizon of sand where brown stops and the Atlantic flats begin and skies begin to rise wet once more.

But not in the field to my west, not any year ever again. Ink started wounding it on a first bill of sale in 1968, and then more ink on more bills (three times in one year once), while profits bloomed from the contracts and rolled over in a mulch of lawyers, agents, and speculators. Each year the large question as to whether it would be farmed went up and down Main Street.

And then one winter in the mid-seventies large, bright rented cars rolled through the field, randomly scattering wintering geese. Strangers sat fogging the glass or got out dressed in the most improbable clothes and pointed. Day after day, up and down my drive, the dark blue and the black cars with whitewalls, doors slamming. Agents, brimming with good will, made the most flourishing gestures (rather like sweeps of the cavalier introducing audience to players, singers to orchestra), their gloved hands flashing above the empty winter stubble as if gathering all of the homes and the lands and the gardens of Sagaponack, which too were part of the vibrant tableau offered for sale.

The field was done in. Wooden sticks sprayed Day-Glo orange gored the earth, and red rags and flags were tied to the branches of the hedgerow. Concrete columns called "monuments" were slipped into the outlines of the plats. . . .

Once achieved, the tenacious hold of place on the heart of the gardener is hard to uproot. Even when forces beyond their control change the nature of place, gardeners at least have nature as their unpredictable, but nevertheless willing, partner. Dash therefore did not move to some other, less-impacted corner of Long Island; rather he chose to shield from view the second homes occupying the former field by planting a double-thick hedge of privet. He laments the loss of his old view of the steeple of the Presbyterian Church of Bridgehampton, but still he continues his long love affair with Madoo, safe in the knowledge that there is one powerful part of the landscape that developers cannot destroy: the moisture-laden, pearly, Atlantic light casting its luminous haze over the garden—something his painter's eye appreciates keenly.

Painting is about color as well as light, and Dash's sensibility as a painter to nuances of hue serves him as well in the garden. He tells us how he reveled at first in a riot of color and a rampancy of vegetation. After this period of "billy-goat bliss," however, he settled down to a more chaste approach to color:

> Over a quarter of a century later, I am perhaps more circumspect. What is here now is mainly green garden. Foliant umbrage is silvery and cottony below and lanced, blunted, toothed, or indented; strap, ovate, and round; margined with white and yellow or speckled silver. Matte or shiny satisfaction take sun, wind, and wet, beginning ruby or tourmaline in spring and echoing them in autumn. The livery is so grave and complete and calming that I wish I were an herbivore. What is it if not superb glissando, rows of unornamented pewter plate on a dark wooden table or emerald crystals carving the very air? Bloom is an afterthought. Almost an impertinence. . . .

What I do may not be for others. We all practice seduction in unique fashion. Yet my heart leans on green, for it is a world-class color, at once oasis and Eden. We agree, don't we, that the green gardens of the Italian Renaissance are unrivaled, unless by that most nearly perfect garden since . . . Rousham? "Green, green," said Lorca. "I would have you green/green hair/green branches." I take green to be not only the predominant color of a flourishing garden but the emblem of its aspiration, the barometer of its health, the very mirror of its finish. Green is its basic architecture clothed, which then becomes its ever-changing form. Great gardens have been green all through, with grass walks and mossed and vined walls enclosing generous, remarkably clipped yews like a great green house of grand green rooms roofed by the light and sky. Green is the color that springs to mind when we think of Eden and the color one most anticipates as a garden is approached.

But his is no Italianate garden where only weathered stone is the counterpoint to green vegetation, and Dash the colorist is very much present. In his case, however, it is "the garden's inanimates—fences, railings, bowls, posts, arbors, doors, gates, benches, and tools—[that] . . . wear high hues of the sort that would make indoor eyeballs wince but were quite suitable outside." And white—this color that is not really a color—he exempts from his censure of all the "seductive frailties" of other colors:

> White gates and benches and houses which are almost like canvas not yet covered, or the blaze in Cézanne watercolors. A white clematis on an old piece of chipping white fence, pouring over and falling through a white rose. An enormous *soulieana*

rose against hedge privet in bloom is a second bit of deliberate engineering I have tried and liked, and that annually works to great satisfaction. And wild daisies are making marvelous stops and explosions throughout the garden and in the fields, glinting like felled clouds or crumbs of our mostly white, monitoring summer skies.

One must, nevertheless, be discriminating in choosing the right floral pigment, and not every white flower will perform the way you think it will. Dash cautions:

> White is composed of all colors, and white flowers tend to waver back into faded memories of their components, no longer true, a blurry thing in the background of an old snapshot becoming curiously defined, almost prominent. White flowers readily go bone in the sun, or tin, or a pale tin running tan, or go gray generally suffused with pink. Each year I plant so-called white Italian sunflowers and they are really pale yellow, but then, I remember, so is macaroni on the plate but rarely in its illustration on the box, and white Italian sunflowers are white only in the photograph on the seed package, as white as the white of white roses shining in catalogues of roses. I cannot recall how many white roses I have planted and tried against blue cypress, gray shingle, black-green yew, and all have been pasta yellow, pretty close to flour mixed with egg. They open in the morning looking old.

But wait. Can any true gardener turn a completely cold shoulder to the rose? One can indeed if they are the scentless modern ones that are annually hybridized primarily for their wow factor as flower-show prize contestants. Given names like 'Perfect Moment', 'Dolly Parton', and 'Tahitian Sunset', they are *meant* to be despised by gardeners like Dash. But not

'Souvenir de la Malmaison', the tender, blush-pink, Bourbon offspring bred in France in 1843 and named for the garden of the Empress Josephine. Dash adores it and can't live without it:

> It is a magnificent rose, pink—the pink we call the cheeks of Renoir children, although they are red. It is a leaping trout pink, this rose. And the petal power of the four-inch flowers stuccoed along extremely well arched stems, loaded to the ground, will cover a wide area and leave you a bit short of breath when they're all out and just beginning to scatter. Let them; don't sweep them up, for they go into a nice musty linen color when they dry and are equally fine.

It is a rose so fine, indeed, that it is worth going to considerable lengths to protect it against the winter harshness of Zone 7. Dash's prescription for how to give 'Souvenir de la Malmaison' the best possible start:

> Peg the stems down wherever they touch the earth. Make a tweezer by splitting a garden bamboo stake, or if you have a nice rock, then a bit of earth and the rock on top will do. During the growing season, the canes will strike root. Should winter kill the host plant, one or two of these will remain quick and will flower true and you will be able to continue enjoying Josephine's *nuit d'amour*. A constant, undisturbed mulch of salt hay placed each autumn around and under the main plant, decently manured on top, will be all the winter preparation and major nutrition it will require.

But just because he loves this "old rose" beauty, it should not be considered as a special feature but "should relate to the whole scheme of your garden and never be placed in a spot of undue prominence." A further stricture: "Roses are always coming down with something. I don't spray and you mustn't spray. In our part of the world, everything put on top of the earth quickly enters our drinking water. Unchanged."

As prickly and prejudiced as Perényi, were he to write the entry under "F" in her book, it would be as a diatribe against forsythia:

> It is an absolute ass of a color, a greeny-yaller braying insult to the obscure triumph of chartreuse, indisputably wrong for spring, or any other season, for that matter—an irritant of March and April along with inflated, dropsical pansies and sundaes of hybrid azaleas dripping over their mulches of co-coa shells. (Our native azaleas are splendid and rarely used.) The heart of forsythia must be made of aluminum, I think. In a cool spring it blooms on and on. Yet in a warmer one, its performance is no less vulgar, for overly robust foliage then smothers it, green yards of it and all crying "Weed!" It does have a single decent moment when the metallic blos-soms drop in little collapses from the stem, sapless and dry and papery dull, coating the ground and making potpourris of little wind-devils across the greening lawn. It is so nice then. Then it seems to rise and sail away into the heart of the spring season, whose hallmark is speed and brevity. All of its other appearances are crude. Its bark is undistinguished. The toothed leaves, although blessedly disease- and insect-free, are as coarse as plantain and look fit only for boiling. Where its branches touch earth—and they do, all the time—they root. Severed roots send up new candidates. Bad and obstinate vines lodge in its base, impossible to eliminate.

We should not leave Madoo without listening to Dash com-plain about the gardener's universal scourge, the repulsive slug tracing its glutinous trail across his book's page. Like Celia Thaxter and Reginald Arkell's "Lady with the Lamp," when heavy mulching has given the slugs a perfect ecological niche in the vegetable garden, Dash sallies forth in darkness as they go about their destructive nocturnal business "to pick off the slimy miserables and drop them in jars of salted water." The reward, however, is worth the effort: "The vegetable garden has returned to its flourishing condition. Salads are simple and uncomplicated matters, leaves taken from the outer bouquet of the plants, a few eaten while picking, the flavor of cold wet dew on a morning lettuce leaf better than coffee or grapefruit juice and toast and jam."

Teachers in the Garden

❦❦

ROFESSIONAL landscape designers are more apt to display their work in lavishly illustrated, large-format volumes with beautiful photographs of gardens they have designed than to produce works that fall into the category of garden writing. Their books may be inspirational visual experiences but not especially educational if you are your own garden-maker looking for fundamental design principles, plant knowledge, and practical advice. Only rarely does one find a garden designer's book that can be classified as both good literature and helpful instruction.

Russell Page

The Education of a Gardener (1962) by Russell Page (1906–1985) is such a book. A memoir in which personal reminiscence, bits of garden history, and numerous original landscape-design suggestions are seamlessly blended, the title reflects its dual nature: a reflection on Page's own learning process and his desire to impart lessons that will teach by example. The fact that the title is "The Education of a Gardener," rather than "The Education of a Garden Designer" is subtly important, for even though he did design gardens, the author never veers from being a man for whom the *act* of gardening is an imperative, with the garden itself being merely the outcome.

In creating gardens for a number of wealthy, famous, and socially prominent clients in the years before World War II, Page developed an idiom that was, above all, responsive to the specifics of place. His first considerations were inevitably topography, climate, existing vegetation, and cultural context. Forced to abandon designing gardens while serving in the Second World War—and, incidentally, at the same time furthering his own education by becoming acquainted with gardens outside the familiar European orbit—he came back to his profession with an understanding of how garden design would henceforth be a matter of working on an altered, smaller scale. Choosing a separate path from that of his modernist contemporaries who had adopted a functionalist ideology, Page based his design philosophy on his own abiding passion for fostering the relationship among plants, nature, architectural forms, and people. Landscape design was for him, first and foremost, an act that occurs in the most literal sense from the ground up. "I have always tried," he says in *The Education of a Gardener*, "to shape gardens each as a harmony, linking people to nature, house to landscape, the plant to its soil." He maintained quite simply that "A good garden cannot be made by somebody who has not developed the capacity to know and to love growing things."

Well before landscape architects practiced on the global scale that some do today, Page was designing gardens in France, Belgium, Switzerland, Italy, and the eastern United States, as well as in his native England. He even had undertaken commissions in Egypt and Persia. Lacking the kind of credentials expected today was hardly a problem, and certainly not one in his eyes. For Page, education was a matter of both seeing and doing. For his purposes it would have been irrelevant and counterproductive to have trained formally in a school of landscape architecture had such an opportunity been available to him.

" 'Book learning' gave me information," he wrote, "but only physical contact can give any real knowledge and understanding of a live organism." Not surprisingly, his earliest and most influential book learning came from the public library. There he "found friends and teachers in Reginald Farrer with his *English Rock Garden* and Gertrude Jekyll with *Wall and Water Gardens*, two people who had spent a lifetime with plants and gardens." He was a capable draftsman and always drew plans, but it was only by walking a site many times over that Page, often in consultation with his clients, was able to achieve his vision for a particular garden—a vision that was organic in every sense of the word. Style for him was always a matter of arranging spaces and objects so as to create an integral composition, something that required an understanding of structure, scale, form, color, texture, and ornament as well as knowledge of the physical characteristics and growth habit of plants. He tells his reader, "I think that awareness of the interplay between objects, whether organic or inorganic, is of major importance if your garden is to be also a work of art." That design ideas were freely borrowed from other cultures did not matter: his gardens were never eclectic pastiches but

rather cultural evocations in which his own fundamental design principles and sense of the fittingness of specific foreign
influences to place and purpose remained paramount.

Sounding the same note as Wharton and Sitwell, Page
speaks of "garden magic." He too looked for it in Italian villa
gardens, reveling in their most magical property, water, and
often exploring their furthest recesses to trace the source of
a pool, rill, or cascade in a hidden spring or grotto. Devoting
a chapter to "Water in the garden," he recalls the sight of Is-
fahan where, "on the western edge of the high Asian Plateau
water is queen." Here "a tiny stepped canal runs down the
middle of the plane-shaded Charhabagh, perhaps the world's
loveliest processional way, and almost every garden is set
symmetrically round a central pool whose four subsidiary rills
carry water into each quarter of the garden and then to the
roots of every tree and plant." As is the case with Wharton
and Sitwell, the point of such observations is to teach a lesson
about the kind of magic that can be applied to one's own making of a garden. But, with more practical pedagogic specificity
than either of them, Page instructs you to observe:

> One of the secrets of using running water successfully and nat-
> urally in a garden is to avoid forcing it into cascades or foun-
> tains which would be at variance with the surrounding land-
> scape. A fountain or jet is apt to look out of place in a garden
> unless there is a hill somewhere to suggest, at least, that your
> jet is expressing the force of water coming from still higher
> ground. For the same reason a fountain or a small pond does
> not usually look right sheer against a background of sea or lake.
> In either case it will appear gratuitous or even pretentious.

Only briefly at the age of eighteen, and much later as an adult when he had a small plot behind a London townhouse, did Page have a garden of his own. After a time of avid self-schooling on a corner of his father's estate in Lincolnshire, his further education was all gained from designing other people's gardens and looking with a discerning eye at many of the humble and noble, simple and grand gardens of the world. As he says in his introduction, "I never saw a garden from which I did not learn something and seldom met a gardener who did not, in one way or another, help me." It is fitting, therefore, that in the final chapter of *The Education of a Gardener*, titled "My Garden," Page allows himself to fantasize about what kind of garden he would in fact make for himself, were he able to choose any site he wished.

Not surprisingly, it would be a garden in England. Since it would be his personal garden, he would have "a workroom with one wall all window, and below it a wide work table running its whole length with a place to draw and a place to write." This room would have whitewashed walls, a brick floor, and an entire wall for books. Outside the window Page imagines an experimental garden of square beds, each of which "will be autonomous, its own small world in which plants will grow to teach me more about their aesthetic possibilities and their cultural likes and dislikes." This will be, he says, "my art gallery of natural forms, a trial ground from which I will always learn, [the place where] I shall find, living and growing, the coloured expansions of my pleasures as a painter and gardener, as well as an addict of catalogues and dictionaries." Leaving this practical corner, he then takes us on a walk through all the passages of this garden of fancy in the same way that Gertrude Jekyll might conduct us around Munstead Wood, a tour in which the lessons of the preceding pages of his book coalesce into a verbal picture. Then at the end Page gives himself up to dreaming of entirely different landscapes and sets of conditions under which to construct other imaginary garden castles in the air. Here lies the final lesson of this remarkable book: like real gardens, dream gardens are worlds unto themselves, "dimensioned in time as well as space; where each leaf, though long since dead and withered, burgeons again and the gossamer web for ever catches the dew of a morning long since past."

Penelope Hobhouse

$\mathcal{P}$enelope Hobhouse's (b. 1929) career as a garden designer began with the restoration of the gardens at Hadspen, her former husband's ancestral home in Somerset. In the introduction to her first book, *The Country Gardener* (1976), she acknowledges the extent to which Margery Fish, who lived nearby, gave her moral support and many stimulating ideas. Like Fish's books, which were her personal garden primers on herbaceous plants, Hobhouse's have since tutored a new generation of garden-makers. Along with the late Rosemary Verey, she has carried forth the long Arts and Crafts garden tradition begun by Gertrude Jekyll—a garden style that glories in the interplay between the architecture of green hedges, mellow stone walls, old brickwork, and the painterly effects achieved by an experienced and imaginative eye for plant color and form. In its relaxed sophistication—a rendition of the cottage garden writ large—it is a quintessentially English style, one that is aided by the advantages of climate and long tradition. Contemporary gardeners who practice and perpetuate it are indebted to Sissinghurst and Hidcote, the two twentieth-century gardens that famously pioneered the paradigm of the garden as a series of hedge-enclosed "rooms." Like their creators, Hobhouse is first and foremost a plant person who uses an in-depth knowledge of the forms, textures, and colors related to seasonal blooming times to make a garden interesting year-round.

Acknowledging the effects on the English garden of waning national economic prosperity, the austerity imposed by two world wars, exponentially higher taxes, and a shortage of labor, Hobhouse's no-nonsense advice is this:

> Achievement of beauty alone is not worth the overstraining of physical strength or financial resources and we should cut our cloth according to our means. Limited labour and limited income now make it necessary for us to practice less costly ways of gardening than those of some of our predecessors, even if we have the same area to maintain. Most of our planting schemes, after an initial period for establishment, should be designed to save maintenance costs and effort. Within that context we can please ourselves as to our specialist enthusiasms.

Before looking at how Hobhouse's seven-acre garden at Hadspen and her familiarity with other English gardens have enhanced her design skills and knowledge of the growing habits of plants, it is worth pausing a moment to glance backward. Reginald Arkell's fine novel *Old Herbaceous* (1951), set in the twilight of the era when head gardeners presided over large estates, provides a benchmark for assessing the descending fortunes of the great nineteenth-century English gardens.

The Garden at Hadspen

From the Peach Walk at Hadspen, the view reaches out into the countryside beyond the garden. Planting in the foreground is framed by older trees and shrubs growing at a lower level. In the border are mauve-flowered *Erysimum linifolium,* Phlox 'Chattahoochee,' and *Geranium sylvaticum* 'Mayflower,' together with silver-leaved *stachys.*

Instructive too in this regard are PBS Masterpiece television productions and Merchant and Ivory movies that portray English gardens in their Edwardian glory days. Swept away by World War I were Picturesque pleasure grounds; rolling fields bounded by wooded brakes from which dogs flushed foxes for hunters; ornamental planting beds with changing seasonal displays of annuals in bloom; conservatories for exotic ferns and palms; hothouses for out-of-season-fruits, vegetables, and tropical flora; cutting gardens for flowers to decorate the rooms of great houses; and kitchen gardens to furnish food for house parties of twenty or more guests. These upper-class landscape and horticultural luxuries were superseded at first by the Arts and Crafts and Italianate gardens of the early years of the twentieth century, which introduced gardening on a somewhat reduced but nevertheless impressive scale. With head gardeners a vanishing breed, there was more owner involvement in the planning and maintaining of gardens. The years leading up to and following World War II saw further curtailment of maintenance staff. This and the vanishing of large family fortunes sparked the creative reinvention of the English garden within even more constricted boundaries, notable examples from this era being Margery Fish's East Lambrook and Vita Sackville-West and Harold Nicolson's Sissinghurst. After the wartime hiatus and under economic constraints that enforced a high degree of practicality, the English genius for gardening as an art form continued to reassert itself, but now even more ingenuity was necessary to produce the renaissance that continues to the present day.

Thus Hobhouse's mission in *The Country Gardener* is to teach other gardeners the cloth-cutting principles of small-scale gardening. Sensible considerations of garden size and the necessary degrees of maintenance upkeep actually encourage experimentation with the ever-wider number of plant varieties available from nurseries. The result has been horticultural creativity as a chief mode of artistic expression. Dismissing the environmentalist argument that gardens should serve as preserves for endangered native plant species, Hobhouse says she feels "entitled to benefit from the discovery of foreign plant material and of methods of using it." Accordingly:

> Our skill lies in interpreting and assessing the relative merits
> of the bewildering choice of garden plants and styles, and in
> acquiring the necessary experience to adapt the use of them
> to our own very individual needs and possibilities. A garden
> is not just a collection of plants; it is the planner's interpre-
> tation of their historical significance and their suitability,
> aided by the experience of the plantsman who understands
> the habits and requirements of the individual plant.

The Country Gardener harks back to the garden books of J. C. and Jane Loudon as well as Louise Beebe Wilder in that its chapters list and describe several botanical species and varieties in each of the categories under consideration. With Hobhouse's commentary on plant histories and recommendations as to their growth habits and where they are best placed in the garden, the book in effect constitutes a primer for the amateur planner of a small site.

Unlike her later books, which were published after four-color printing became common, the first edition of *The*

Country Gardener has only meager black-and-white illustrations. Those who read it as they would a nursery catalogue, hoping to visualize how certain plants will look in their own gardens, would like more and better pictures specific to each of her plant profiles. However, Hobhouse's careful descriptions laced with fillips of botanical information go a good way toward making up in words for this lack of images. Here is how she writes about the tulip tree in a chapter titled "Form-Giving Trees and Shrubs for Garden Design":

> *Liriodendron. L. tulipifera* is a well known and very handsome tree from North America which has been grown in this country since the seventeenth century. No garden of more than half an acre should be without one. Its fine straight trunk branches into a spreading head and balances suitability with any groupings of buildings or with other trees. It makes very little shade and has distinctive leaves and flowers. The leaves have flattened ends like broad fish-tails, and the flowers are tulip-shaped and greenish-yellow. The foliage becomes quite pale after the first frosts. There are many good examples of this tree, notably at Stourhead in Wiltshire. There is also an attractive variegated form. *Liriodendron chinense* was introduced from China by Ernest Wilson in 1901; I have never seen it but am greatly tempted to try one as the Asian varieties of so many genera are superior to the North American ones, and many of my favorite plants seem to have been introduced to the West by 'Chinese Wilson' as he was called—hence the '*sino-wilsoni*' found in plant epithets.

In *The Country Gardener* Hobhouse does a particularly good job of delivering easy-to-understand condensations of specialized horticultural information. Her synopsis on the properties of soil is a good example. Those who are confused about the meaning in terms of garden requirements of a certain pH factor—a figure expressing the acidity or alkalinity of soil (or other chemical matter) on a logarithmic scale, with 7 as neutral and lower values increasingly acidic and higher ones more alkaline—can learn that rhododendrons, azaleas, camellias, and other ericaceous plants need acidic soil to thrive and that the addition of lime will sweeten such soil into the desirable level of alkalinity needed by other kinds of plants. Three more pages is all it takes for her to walk us through soil texture and workability and their effect on drainage; the various types of soil (with a natural mixture of sand, silt, and clay in well-balanced proportions being "every gardener's dream"); and the varying ratios of the principal mineral elements (nitrogen, phosphorus, and potassium) fertilizer must have in order to enrich soil in species-specific ways.

There is another helpful chapter on ground covers, and one on roses as shrubs. Here Hobhouse reverently refers to the man who is widely acknowledged as the doyen of roses: "Not only has Graham Stuart Thomas been responsible for saving and preserving many of the old roses which are the ancestors of the modern hybrid teas and floribundas, but he has also written extensively about them." We are reminded here of E. A. Bowles directing his readers to the "Moraine Magician," Reginald Farrer, when Hobhouse urges hers "to go to the fountain-head of knowledge, the books of Mr. Stuart Thomas" for comprehensive advice.

But before going into a highly selective list of the hardy, disease-resistant shrub roses she herself has grown, Hobhouse provides an economical précis of the history of the rose and its many mutations through hybridization. It is a story with certain erotic overtones. At the outset there was "the Gallica rose which has been known and cultivated in Asia since the beginning of history." Crossed with the musk rose, this ur-rose became the damask, which arrived in Europe with the Crusaders, where crossed with the dog rose, it produced the *alba* group and later the *centifolias*, of which the moss rose is a sport dating from the eighteenth century. The introduction of the rugosa rose from Japan occurred in 1796, a hundred years after the China rose, the ancestor of all repeat-flowering roses. Hobhouse then informs us that "in 1823 the China rose made an accidental alliance with the Autumn Damask, in Reunion Island (then called Isle de Bourbon) in the Indian Ocean." The result of this promiscuous act was the Bourbon rose, which, when crossed with one of its relatives, gave birth to the hybrid perpetuals, with their recurrent flowering. Following this, we learn: "The delicate Tea rose came from China in 1867 and its introduction in the West led to an orgy of crossing and re-crossing, which led to the modern Hybrid Teas and subsequently the Floribundas." More Asian introductions at the turn of the twentieth century led to more interbreeding, with the result that gardeners today have a hard time discriminating among the kinds of roses that will please them most and thrive best in the circumstances provided.

After her first marriage ended in 1983, Hobhouse left Hadspen to take charge of the gardens at Tintinhull House, the National Trust property where she lived and worked with her second husband, John Malins, until 1993. Hosting a television program in 1996 and publishing a spate of books brought her considerable renown in the gardening world, along with consulting requests and invitations to lecture. At the same time, she became much in demand as an international garden designer. Her work in England, Scotland, France, Germany, Italy, Spain, and the United States added to her prestige. Her talents were formally recognized with the Royal Horticultural Society's Victoria Medal of Honour in 1996 and the Lifetime Achievement award from the Guild of Garden Writers in 1999.

In 2008 Hobhouse moved back to Hadspen, where she started a new garden adjacent to the smaller house on the estate where she now lives. Summing up her career and philosophy, she says:

> The overall success of a design is really to do with how someone has manipulated space. It is often supposed that women find it very much more difficult to deal with three-dimensional space and the transformation of its contours on a large scale while they are much better at editing and complex colour associations. This may generally be true, but of course designers have to do both. As time has passed, I have become less interested in the close-up, in the individual plant (although an interesting new plant with character is always stimulating) and I am more and more interested in the broader picture, the wider landscape.

Rosemary Verey

Like Penelope Hobhouse, Rosemary Verey (1918–2001) earned a wide reputation as a self-taught gardener and garden designer, as well as the author of eighteen books on gardens. Although indebted, as was Hobhouse, to what might be called the Gertrude Jekyll school of gardening, in her books Verey reveals a more architectonic approach. This does not imply, however, that she was not equally adept at composing an array of plants in such combinations as to display the changing seasonal appearance of the garden to best advan-

Temple and Pool, Rosemary Verey's garden at Barnsley House.

tage. Indeed, it was she who influenced Hobhouse's style of gardening and brought her work to public recognition in her first book, *The Englishwoman's Garden* (1980).

"Structure" is a word Verey often employed, and a garden's lines—its axial views and its paths—are important concepts in her design vocabulary. At the same time, tight control of plant forms was hardly her objective: rather than static perfection, surprise and serendipity—happy accidents such as fortuitous self-seeding within a clear design framework—are evident in the garden she and her husband David Verey, an architectural historian, created at Barnsley House near Cirencester. One might liken their collaboration in establishing the garden's "bones" within the footprint of David's parents' garden to that of Harold Nicolson and Vita Sackville-West's laying out of Sissinghurst. However, while the gardens at Barnsley House reveal a similar combination of David's "classicism" and Rosemary's "romanticism," the Vereys' taste did not gravitate toward a series of hedge-enclosed garden rooms, but rather to a more open plan with orchestrated views from one section of the garden to another.

Rosemary Verey's Making of a Garden (1995) is both the autobiography of a gardener and the story of how she and David, who was given Barnsley House by his parents in 1951, created the garden. It is remarkable that this garden adjacent to an unassuming three-story William and Mary house built by a country squire in 1697, could become a cynosure attracting a stream of 30,000 visitors a year. Its popularity as a pilgrimage spot for serious gardeners is due in part to Verey's rise from amateur gardener to self-trained garden designer, successful garden-book author, and much-in-demand lecturer both in England and America. As with the other books considered here whose titles have the word "making" in them, what fascinates the reader is the story of the garden's development over time as its maker grows in botanical, horticultural, and design skill.

According to her biographer, Barbara Paul Robinson, Verey's passion for gardening began with her collection of old herbals. Her fascination with rare books on botany and garden history contributed to her desire to become an active gardener. They also helped form her taste for classic design, in which form and structure provided by geometrical layouts and the division of the garden into discrete but linked parts were as important as the seasonal appearance and growing habits of flowers, shrubs, and trees. Robinson, herself an accomplished gardener who took a sabbatical from her law practice in order to apprentice herself to Verey, says, "Rosemary was a marvelous teacher and a great plantsperson. She was always an encourager, an educator of others, and very generous in promoting the reputations of other gardeners."

Like Russell Page, Verey had a strong following in the United States, where she designed several gardens. In Britain her client roster included such notables as HRH the Prince of Wales, Sir Elton John, and Princess Michael of Kent. She was friends with several distinguished professional landscape designers and occasionally collaborated with some of them. Along with other contemporary gardeners who employ a sophisticated plant palette whereby green architectural structure serves as a foil for casual-seeming horticultural luxuriance, she was a particular friend of Christopher Lloyd.

Although not as prolific a garden writer as Verey, whose spate of garden books appeared at annual intervals, Lloyd deserves more than a passing reference. His garden surrounding Great Dixter, a timber-framed Elizabethan manor enlarged by Sir Edwin Lutyens's addition of an Arts and Crafts-style house, is by several accounts the finest modern-day example of innovative garden artistry wedded to England's time-honored rural landscape. More than an amanuensis, Fergus Garrett, Great Dixter's talented head gardener and current caretaker, worked for several years alongside Christo—as Lloyd was known to his many admiring friends—and therefore shares some of the credit for the garden's striking originality and deeply expressive alliance with the surrounding fields of hops and the oast houses in which they are dried.

Paying tribute to Lloyd's horticultural artistry, Verey wrote:

Christopher must be the number one influence on the late twentieth-century generation of gardeners—a brilliant plantsman, full of imaginative ideas. At Great Dixter in Sussex he inherited the care of a structured garden created by his parents, and his genius lies in his ever-vital planting thoughts. He loves berries, shapes, skeletons mingled with evergreens and he helped me to realize that my garden is as important in winter as it is in June. His stimulating articles each week in *Country Life* constantly make us aware that adjacent colours which (I think) clash, should have a place in every garden. So now we have shell-pink *Oenothera speciosa* . . . growing with orange eschscholzias from California. They both seed themselves where they flank a path and are contained within two lines of box edging only 30 centimeters/12 inches apart. Every time I walk along this path I think of him and remember that gardening must be fun.

In America, Verey admired the originality of Robert Dash, whose boldly eccentric creativity as a garden-maker on Long Island won from her this praise:

Years ago I was told, 'It is a sin to be dull.' Having met Bob Dash and basked in the originality of his garden in Long Island, I can comprehend the meaning. Bob has very clear-cut, artistic and original ideas about his gardens. He is primarily an artist and his garden is designed with a bravado which most of us lack. He also paints in bold swathes but plants with a delicate touch—our own 'Bob Dash' bed is my tribute to his planting style. His gates, doors, and fences are in colours unusual in a garden, all geared to the appropriate season.

Christopher Lloyd's garden at Great Dixter.

And back home in England, she enthused:

I bow to David Hicks for his clearly defined theories. He has surrounded his house with a new garden of interrelated spaces dependent upon his instinctive eye for form. He has taught me the importance of using different mowing heights and of linking each space to create a natural flow and also a change of mood, sometimes simply relying on the infinite variety of the colour green.

Written as a companion book for a BBC television series she hosted, her last book, *Rosemary Verey's English Country Gardens* (1996), deals with the gardens of the wealthy and famous as well as those of distinguished garden-makers such as Lloyd. Here, her treatment of her subjects, several of whom were her clients, is more praising than disparaging, as might be expected, and she presents herself as student as much as authority:

> A lesson I learnt from the late Countess Münster's garden at Bampton is the importance of planting narcissus in drifts of the same variety, so colours are not mixed. If spaces are left between them for other features to come on later, these will direct your attention from the dying daffodil leaves. Christo in his meadow has early purple orchids, *Orchis mascula*, and the spotted orchid, *Dactylorhiza fuchsii*. Both of these will self-sow if the seeds fall in an undisturbed place.
>
> In May the dominant flower in the entrance meadow is *Camassia quamash*, a 60 cm (2 ft) tall blue flowered bulb native to the north-west of America. Christopher first planted these many years ago when they were comparatively cheap and easy to get—now Prince Charles has them in his meadow garden where they flower at the same time as the dark purple tulip 'The Bishop'. Christo's have increased—I hope those at Highgrove will do the same.

History and celebrity cohere at Woodside:

> The decision as to whether or not you can say 'yes' to a prospective client is often difficult. When Elton John's personal assistant, Robert Key, rang me and mentioned the name 'Woodside', my thought immediately turned to the mid-eighteenth-century artist Thomas Robins, who specialized in painting English rococo gardens. Sure enough in John Harris' book *Gardens of Delight* (published in 1978) were watercolours showing Woodside gardens in the 1650s. In America I found a copy of the limited edition, which I bought for Elton.

She then proceeds to give the reader an imaginary walking tour of the garden she made in collaboration with the freelance designers Gordon Taylor and Guy Cooper within the footprint of the old, eighteenth-century rococo garden at Woodside. About the pool that they created in the woodland, she comments:

> Seeing this pool in spring, I was full of hope that Elton finds time to walk here when he is home. Now there is a perfect way into the woodland, over the wooden bridge framed by two old oak trees, and soon you come to this pool. You can walk all round it, as we did. As we wandered on, Helen [the head gardener] said, 'Well, you never know what you're going to find in a wood like this', we rounded a corner—and there was a fiberglass dinosaur, 'Daisy', looking as though she was about to spring out of the undergrowth.
>
> When Daisy first arrived at Woodside, as a present from George Harrison, she was isolated on the lawn with no planting around her. My reaction was that she must find her way into the woodland—a more appropriate setting for her. She moved in by helicopter, cleverly arranged by Guy

and Gordon. It must have been a bit of a shock for her, and now she duly responds by surprising visitors, especially after dark when an infra-red sensor is automatically set to light her up. Helen and her gardeners did good work with the planting around her. There are *Trachycarpus fortunei*, variegated phormium and *Nandina domestica* amongst the laurels. It is important to keep the mystery with enough appropriate shrubs close by, but her full size must be visible, from her tail to her large back legs and her glittering eye.

Tempted to give a nod of approval to the design team for their clever transfer of this oversize piece of kitsch from the open lawn to the secluded woodland, we might also remember that eighteenth-century rococo gardens were themselves filled with exotic follies intended to amaze visitors.

More satisfying to the tactful Verey in all probability was Folly Farm, the great Lutyens house and Jekyll garden in Berkshire. As at Great Dixter, here Lutyens grafted a beautiful Arts and Crafts house onto an earlier farmhouse, and Jekyll prepared the planting plans for the garden. Verey writes:

> On a warm summer's morning Emily Lucy Astor and I started our walk round the garden from the front door of the old farmhouse, which leads into the two barn courts. Here is a feeling of an enclosed cottage garden. What first struck me were the two straight paths, unmistakably designed by Sir Edwin Lutyens, with narrow bricks laid in a herringbone pattern and edged with cut stone. . . . Also characteristic of a Lutyens garden are the enticing seats. Emi-Lu and I had reached the terrace, enclosed on three sides by house walls, and here Hugh Astor was waiting for us. I was longing to

hear more about their achievements in the garden since 1951, and their opinion as to how strictly a Gertrude Jekyll planting should be followed.

Today there is much discussion and controversy about the principles of garden restoration. Should planting be historically correct, or can new plants be added, as surely the owner and designer would have done today? This is a pertinent question at Folly Farm. Hugh explained that they have had to simplify the garden, and also that they have used more modern plants than were available to Gertrude Jekyll: 'I do feel it's a living thing and has to change with the time and the wishes of the owners. Surely a garden shouldn't be fossilized?'

Verey, who was awarded the OBE in 1996 and the Victoria Medal of Honour from the Royal Horticultural Society in 1999, clearly represents the post-World War II renaissance in English gardening. Upkeep on great estates like Chatsworth, seat of the Duke of Devonshire, is funded in part by auxiliary revenue-producing ventures, and many smaller gardens such as Sissinghurst and Hidcote Manor survive only by virtue of being National Trust properties. Margery Fish's East Lambrook Manor Gardens, which are managed by a private trust, charge admission, and plants sold from the nursery also help support their upkeep. Several years before her death, Verey moved into the Close next to Barnsley House, which, like William Robinson's Gravetye Manor, now serves as an upscale country hotel where Richard Gatenby, Verey's head gardener, continues to maintain the gardens she and her husband created over the course of half a century.

Linda Yang

That the city gardener faces more challenges than the country gardener should be obvious. In *The City Gardener's Handbook: The Definitive Guide to Small-Space Gardening* (2002) Linda Yang does not ignore or lightly brush them aside. As a longtime New York City apartment dweller and brownstone owner, she laces advice with personal experience, cheerfully encouraging the reader to look at setbacks as learning opportunities. To lessen disappointments, however, she takes you through the ABCs of what you might like to think of as hardy horticulture. Be advised: "The city gardener is a determined soul who must sow where there are more obstacles and inhabitants than soil"—that is, if you, like her and other true gardeners, derive happiness from creating beauty in spite of your garden's seemingly anomalous situation.

Though tailored to her urban audience, much of Yang's advice applies to all novice gardeners. As a first step she recommends a preliminary conditions assessment in which you determine the amount of sunlight your garden will receive. In addition to noting how it is positioned according to the sun's angle in relationship to the earth's latitude and the cardinal directions, you need to realize that surrounding buildings and tiered terraces on higher floors may cast shadows on it. If you are stuck with a sunless site, don't worry unnecessarily, for Yang has a chapter in which she fulfills her promise to help you choose a plant for *every* condition. You may "rest assured that your seasonal plants can include crocus in the spring, the puckered, oval foliage of hosta in summer, fresh mint in fall and evergreen yews in winter."

Even if you can tolerate shade, however, there are other microclimatic factors to take into account. These include wind conditions, radiant heat, hot-water pipes, improper roof insulation, and whether a clothes-dryer exhaust, oven fan, or some other piece of mechanical equipment is causing a hot spot. If you aren't able to determine these problems in advance, be on a diagnostic lookout for plants that expire for no apparent reason.

And just what plants should you choose once you have assessed your hazards and figured out what kind of architectural embellishment, furnishings, visual camouflage, and tool storage you might need? Here Yang counters the common belief that cities are inhospitable to plants with a long, annotated list of species that can thrive in the urban environment. In addition, she applies her upbeat approach to making novice gardeners comfortable with the Linnaean system of binomial nomenclature. After explaining that capitalized first names refer to the plant's genus (say, *Acer* for maple, *Quercus* for oak), she describes the way in which species' second names are conferred:

> Some botanical names commemorate a person, usually a patron or the plant collector who introduced the species (like *farreri* in honor of Reginald Farrer, or *davidii* for Père Jean Pierre David). Others are descriptive of a flower or leaf outline (*palmatum* for resemblance to an outspread hand, *pendula* for hanging down), leaf or plant size (*nanus* or *pumilus* for small or dwarf), texture (*pubescens* for downy) or color (*purpureum* for purple, *argenteus* for silvery or metallic gray). For

example, a popular Japanese maple for city gardens is *Acer palmatum* 'Atropurpureum.' This plant has red-colored hand-shaped leaves.

Nature knows no boundaries, and as if by magic a host of insects invades the urban garden with as much voracity as the country garden. City slickers are not only amazed but also, as a rule, ignorant of whether a particular insect is destructive or benign. With characteristic breeziness, Yang attacks the subject of pests with simple practicality:

So what's a gardener to do when an unfamiliar insect appears?

Without a degree in entomology, how can you know if there's dirty work afoot?

The answer is *observation*. This is the only tool we amateurs have, and it's a pretty good one.

Watch the creature carefully for a while and see what it's up to. If it seems to be minding its own business and you have no previous evidence to the contrary, guilt should not be presumed—that position, after all, is antithetical to American law.

Remember, too, you can't judge an insect friend by its looks, some important allies have a fearsome visage. Take, for example, that insectivorous monster, the praying mantis. One year, a 3-inch-long mantis settled on my tub of roses. At first my family was unsettled by its grotesque green face, ungainly limbs and truly atrocious table manners (chewing raw insects!), but by summer's end it had become an accepted and most entertaining resident. In retrospect, I can only wonder at my city children, who so casually named their peculiar "pet" *Bob*.

Nevertheless, there are still noxious garden predators that cannot be deterred by praying mantises or any of the other biological pest controls you can now get by mail order. Just how to check their depredations is the problem. Staying at first on environmental high ground, Yang recommends full-force blasting with a watering hose, dousing plants with a soapy spray, applying horticultural oils derived from petroleum hydrocarbons, and using homemade repellents (she passes along a recipe calling for the following ingredients: cigarette tobacco, crushed garlic, household ammonia, and liquid soap). Moving into a more aggressive mode, she advocates "search and destroy" missions. These include "dropping egg masses or cocoons into kerosene, undiluted liquid detergent, or a water-and-ammonia solution." Getting even more creative, she suggests that "you might prefer to knock the beasts into a jar and donate them for 'nature study' to a school," adding that "children might even be induced to do the trapping for you if offered a 'bounty' for every pest caught—but keep the price low; some are tireless workers." At last, like Beverley Nichols, she gives in to chemistry, saying, "When there's no longer a tolerable number of freeloaders and a major invasion is under way, pesticides are acceptable."

No one ever said that gardening wasn't a lot of work, and Yang's almanac of seasonal tasks—moving seedlings and tender overwintered plants outdoors in the spring; pruning, watering, and weeding throughout the summer; planting bulbs, harvesting vegetables, dividing perennials, and putting houseplants back indoors in the fall; mulching, tree pruning, and of course catalogue consulting in the winter—proves the point. These are only the more obvious tasks, ones that apply to all gardeners. City gardeners have additional chores to perform, such as hosing soot off evergreens and repainting the railings of balconies and terraces. But reading Yang, we feel that the pleasure they take in their own bits of urban greenery is worth the effort. Indeed, their enjoyment may be enhanced by all the challenges they face. If you should doubt this, just take a look around Yang's native Manhattan, and you will see gardens everywhere.

Lynden B. Miller

*M*ost of the writers we are discussing here have harvested an abundance of commentary on their home grounds. Lynden B. Miller (b. 1938) could easily have written from the perspective of the garden she made at her second home in Salisbury, Connecticut, but in *Parks, Plants, and People* (2009) she focuses instead on the various gardens she has designed in public spaces. Leaving the high-rise terrace, balcony, rooftop, and brownstone backyard to Yang, her professional turf is the urban park and city square.

Miller's story begins at the Harlem end of Central Park in 1982, in the Conservatory Garden, when she accepted the newly-formed Central Park Conservancy's challenge to restore—or better, to re-create—the tripartite Beaux Arts garden that Commissioner Robert Moses inserted into Frederick Law Olmsted and Calvert Vaux's Romantic landscape in 1936. Her success and the continuing acclaim the garden received encouraged Miller, who was then a painter, to trade in her artist's palette for one comprised of flats of plants.

Just as Jekyll's career as an artist stimulated her to become a maker of garden pictures, Miller's artist's eye has aided her over the past three decades in her creation of several public gardens that adorn parks and campuses in New York City and elsewhere. Their painterly array of ornamental plants would not have thrived under the conditions of heavy use and environmental stress if her designs were not grounded in sound horticultural knowledge. *Parks, Plants, and People* is thus both a tour of several beautified public landscapes and a primer for making garden art, whether public or private.

Throughout she refers to Elizabeth von Arnim, Gertrude Jekyll, Vita Sackville-West, Louise Beebe Wilder, and other earlier garden writers whom she counts as her literary companions and mentors. For instance, in a long chapter titled "The Art of Garden Design," Miller starts off by saying:

> To my eye, the ideal composition is one that looks almost unplanned—but this actually requires careful planning and experience with plants. The great English gardener and writer Vita Sackville-West called this kind of gardening "a kind of haphazard luxuriance, which of course comes neither by hap nor hazard at all," This type of planting may look as if some invisible hand had just dropped the plants here and there, but the effect actually takes considerable organization and definition.

The mixed border— a long bed in which bulbs, perennials, annuals, shrubs, and low-growing trees combine to create a tapestry of plants—is Miller's particular specialty. During the 1970s when she lived in England she looked with an attentive eye at the mixed borders contained within a structural framework of paths, walls, and hedges at Sackville-

West's Sissinghurst, Christopher Lloyd's Great Dixter, and Lawrence Johnston's Hidcote—all places where gardening is demonstrated to be one of the fine arts. Practicing the lessons she learned from these and the gardens of other proponents of this form of garden design—Rosemary Verey and Penelope Hobhouse, to name the most recent—Miller aims to teach her readers how to create compositions of plants that provide visual interest during the four seasons of the year. To do this, of course, requires an approach to gardening as a science in which the variables of time and weather need to be understood. "If you know your plants well," she writes, "you will have no reason to leave a park or garden devoid of plant pleasures in winter. Evergreen foliage, interesting bark, and colorful berries are the joys of the season."

The words "if you know your plants well" are, of course, key. Recalling Jekyll, Miller observes "Many people begin their gardening by thinking that the making and maintaining of a well-filled flower border is quite an easy matter. In fact it is one of the most difficult problems in the whole range of horticultural practice." To plan her borders, Miller thinks of form, texture, and color, giving one section to trees and shrubs, with flowering dogwoods, magnolias, and broad-leaved evergreens such as holly (for winter color) taking front seat; one to perennials, which she calls "the flesh" on the garden's "bones" (here she recommends a host of sun- and shade-loving species, with a nod to her reliable favorites: *Helleborus*, *Alchemilla*, *Anemone*, *Geranium*, *Salvia*, *Sedum*, *Thalictrum*, *Hosta*, and *Yucca*); one to grasses, such as several varieties of *Miscanthus sinensis* along with oat grass (*Helictotrichon sempervirens*) and golden Japanese forest grass (*Hakonechloa macra* 'Aureola'); one to annuals, including a star performer, *Ageratum houstonianum* 'Blue Horizon' (floss flower); one to biennials like *Digitalis* (foxglove); one to bulbs, including *Allium*, the ornamental onion plant; and, finally, one to native plants, with *Hydrangea quercifolia* (oakleaf hydrangea) being her favorite.

Once you have your palette—this means a large catalogue of mental images of plants and an informed sense of their seasonal growth habits—you then need to master the elements of design: foliage contrast, repetition, form, line, scale, and color. Here Miller shows how the large, smooth blue leaves of a hosta contrast with the "thin, yellow-green strappy leaves" of golden Japanese forest grass; how softly undulating grasses repeat the flow of falling water; how the necessary "crisp discipline"

The South Garden, Conservatory Garden, Central Park.

of an edge is softened by the way a plant is allowed to spill over it; how hedges create sight lines and at the same time serve to contain exuberant plantings; how complementary colors such as blue and orange or a single color in many different shades can create an effective design.

Like other good garden writers she cannot omit discussing soil: "Ideally it should be dark brown and smell fresh, and it should make a ball in your hand when you squeeze it. If the soil is in good condition your hands will hold millions of invisible microorganisms, more than there are people on the face of the planet." She recommends soil testing by one's state extension service or a private company; soil amendment to relieve compaction, poor drainage, or nutrient deficiencies; and various types of compost—the gardener's gold—to meet the demands of different kinds of plants.

The North Garden, Conservatory Garden, Central Park.

Public sector gardeners must deal with the same vagaries of weather and infuriating depredations of garden pests as private gardeners. But they have other challenges to overcome as well, which Miller makes clear in a final chapter devoted to the subject. Having on site an enthusiastic trained gardener capable of communicating with the public; selecting the right kinds of plants, preferably ones that are beautiful during at least three seasons; protecting them with unobtrusive temporary fencing while they are getting established; and preventing injurious salt and chemicals used to remove snow on paths from leaching into the soil are just some of the things that must be added to regular good maintenance practices such as watering, weeding, pruning, mulching, and so forth.

Miller believes that public gardens are cynosures of the city and symbols of good urbanism. In this respect, the word "people" in her title is significant. "Well-maintained parks tell people that their city cares about them and give them a compelling reason to remain in the city," she concludes, a belief she affirms with an anecdote:

> A visitor once said to me, after experiencing the Conservatory Garden for the first time, that she had intended to leave New York, but if there was a place like this in the city, she wasn't leaving. . . . With so much to divide us, one thing seems common to us all: everyone loves to be surrounded by something beautiful.

Her motto is "Make it gorgeous and they will come; keep it that way and they will help you."

Philosophers in the Garden

❦

PHILOSOPHY and the garden have a long history of affinity. In the fifth century BCE Socrates conversed with his pupils in a *stoa*— a colonnaded, pergola-like structure in the Athenian agora—and Plato's Academy outside of Athens might be considered a garden prototype for the university campuses of later ages. Natural science was a branch of philosophy from Aristotle until the nineteenth century. For Romantics like Rousseau, Nature (with a capital N) and the garden are inseparable. For those of a philosophical bent, soil, flowers, and garden pests have always served as tropes for larger themes. And for contemporary gardeners, myself included, there are moments when weeding becomes an opportunity for Zen-type meditation rather than simply a chore.

Henry David Thoreau

In his famous essay *Nature* (1836), Ralph Waldo Emerson (1803–1882) enunciated an essentially American philosophy that influenced the thinking of his friend and follower Henry David Thoreau (1817–1862). Although, on an 1832 visit to the Jardin des Plantes in Paris, Emerson displayed an interest in botany, his appreciation of the natural world went well beyond the bounds of Enlightenment science and into the realm of the religious when he proclaimed that "Nature wears the colors of the Spirit." This Romantic attitude embraced the rural landscape of the immediate countryside as well as the solemn forests, for Emerson apprehended divinity in all of nature's manifestations.

Thoreau gave his own interpretation to the message of the great Transcendentalist in *Walden* (1854), and in other essays on the virtues of self-aware communion with the natural world. It was, of course, in the woods near Concord, Massachusetts, that he set up his experimental divorce from society, and his description of that enterprise, as chronicled in *Walden*, is both a diatribe against civilization's stifling conformities and a philosophy that would be promulgated with zeal by environmentalists more than a century later. Because of his Rousseau-like belief in the virtue of primitive nature as an antidote to a life of social constraint, Thoreau's attempt at gardening is instructive. In the chapter called "The Bean Field," he allows how his efforts are not to provide sustenance so much as to find parables in the soil:

> What was the meaning of this Herculean labor, I knew not. I came to love my rows, my beans, though many more than I wanted. They attached me to the earth, and so I got strength like Antaeus. But why raise them? Only Heaven knows. This was a curious labor all summer—to make this portion of the earth's surface, which had yielded only cinquefoil, blackberries, johnswort, and the like, before, sweet wild fruits and pleasant flowers, produce instead of pulse? What shall I learn from beans or they of me? I cherish

them, I hoe them, early and late I have an eye on them; and this is my day's work. It is a fine broad leaf to look on. My auxiliaries are the dews and the rains which water this dry soil, and what fertility is in the soil itself, which for the most part is sterile and effete. My enemies are worms, cool days, and most of all woodchucks. The last have nibbled for me a quarter of an acre clean. But what right had I to oust johns-wort and the rest, and break up their ancient herb garden? Soon, however, the remaining beans will be too tough for them, and go forward to meet new foes.

Thoreau goes on to muse about the previous Native American occupation of his bean field as he turns up arrowheads with his hoe. This causes him to surmise that the prior human occupation and cultivation of beans on the same site "had exhausted the soil for this very crop." Persevering, he tells us how, barefooted in dews in early morning, he "began to level the ranks of haughty weeds . . . and throw dust upon their heads." Reflecting on his continuing transformation of the landscape, he says, "Removing the weeds, putting fresh soil about the bean stems, and encouraging this weed which I had sown, making the yellow soil express its summer thought in bean leaves and blossoms rather than in wormwood and piper and millet grass, making the earth say beans instead of grass—this was my daily work."

But for Thoreau, cultivating his bean field was not drudgery. Like an archaeologist, he continued to discover the remains of ancient occupation. He likens to music the sound of the hoe striking these artifacts and those of later sojourners in these same woods. Rejoicing, he says:

It was no longer beans that I hoed, nor that I hoed beans, and I remembered with as much pity as pride, if I remembered it at all, my acquaintances who had gone to the city to attend the oratorios. The night-hawk circled overhead in the sunny afternoon—for I sometimes made a day of it—and like a mote in the eye, or in heaven's eye, falling from time to time with a swoop and a sound as if the heavens were rent, torn at last to very rags and tatters, and yet a seamless cope remained; small imps that fill the air and lay their eggs on the ground on bare sand or rocks on the tops of hills, where few have found them; graceful and slender like ripples caught up from the pond, as leaves are raised by the wind to float in the heavens; such kindredship is in Nature. . . .

Those summer days which some of my contemporaries devoted to the fine arts in Boston or Rome, and others to contemplation in India, and others to trade in London or New York, I thus, with the other farmers of New England, devoted to husbandry. Not that I wanted beans to eat, for I am by nature a Pythagorean, so far as beans are concerned, whether they mean porridge or voting, and exchanged them for rice; but, perchance, as some must work in fields if only for the sake of tropes and expression, to serve a parable-maker one day. It was on the whole a rare amusement, which, continued too long, might have become a dissipation. . . .

But did he need to bother at all with beans in order to be a moral philosopher and go about the business of sermonizing his readers?

This further experience I gained. I said to myself, I will not plant beans and corn with so much industry another summer, but such seeds, if the seed is not lost, as sincerity, truth, simplicity, faith, innocence, and the like, and see if they will not grow in this soil, even with less toil and manurance, and sustain me, for surely it has not been exhausted by these crops.

There was a further rationale for abandoning his bean field, which might be said to fall under the rubric "The Rights of Weeds." Thoreau now believed that it was nature's prerogative to continue its own vegetal dynamic in the interest of the local wildlife. Reminding us that "the sun shines on our cultivated fields and on the prairies and forests without distinction . . . [and] in his view the earth is all equally cultivated like a garden," he theorized: "These beans have results which are not harvested by me. Do they not grow for woodchucks partly? . . . Shall I not rejoice also at the abundance of the weeds whose seeds are the granary of the birds?" Thus, in Thoreau's philosophy—which sidesteps the subject of agriculture as the primary source of human sustenance—the garden is not a part of nature cultivated for the benefit and pleasure of mankind: Nature *is* the garden, and its own beauty and bounty is the nourishment of the soul.

Michael Pollan

A master of the essay as a literary form, Michael Pollan (b. 1955) is a professor of journalism at the University of California, Berkeley. Nowadays he is best known as an author whose incisive examination of the American system of industrial food production and its alternatives has provoked considerable national attention. For Pollan, the agricultural landscape is the garden writ large, but his entry into this subject of continental dimensions began in his own garden in Cornwall, Connecticut. *Second Nature: A Gardener's Education* (1991)—a series of essays originally published in *Harper's Magazine*, *The New York Times Magazine*, and *The New Yorker*—chronicles both the horticultural and moral lessons he learned in this garden—or rather, the morals inherent in the horticultural lessons he learned from gardening.

It is in the garden that Pollan, like Thoreau, is engaged in a day-to-day contemplation of the complicated relationship between humankind and nature. But Pollan does not necessarily agree with the sage of Walden's romantic view of First Nature, and *Second Nature* is, in effect, an extended debate with Thoreau. For Pollan, civilization and nature are not necessarily oppositional forces; the garden is metaphorically the fruitful middle ground where "nature and culture can be wedded in a way that can benefit both." This idea, he believes, "may be as useful to us today as the idea of wilderness has been in the past."

Like several of the other gardeners we have encountered throughout this book, Pollan displayed his gardening gene in childhood. His discovery of this nascent passion wasn't exactly parallel to Gertrude Jekyll's cultivation of a corner of the family estate in Surrey or the gardens in which Morse and Wilder played as children:

> My first garden was a place no grown-up ever knew about, even though it was in the backyard of a quarter-acre suburban plot. Behind our house in Farmingdale, Long Island, stood a rough hedge of lilac and forsythia that had been planted to hide the neighbor's slat wood fence. My garden, which I shared with my sister and our friends, consisted of the strip of

unplanted ground between the hedge and the fence. To a four-year-old, though, the space made by the vaulting branches of a forsythia is as grand as the inside of a cathedral, and there is room enough for a world between a lilac and a wall. Whenever I needed to be out of range of adult radar, I'd crawl beneath the forsythia's arches, squeeze between two lilac bushes, and find myself safe and alone in my own green room.

What child does not relish taking possession of a leafy enclosure and making invisibility a kind of power? Pollan tells us of his self-defining moment as a gardener-to-be when one day he discovered "a stippled green football sitting in a tangle of vines and broad leaves" and made the connection between the seed he had spit out and shoved in the ground a few months earlier and the watermelon he now beheld. Never mind that the watermelon crashed to the ground as he ran to show it to his mother. "Memories of one kind or another play around the edges of every garden, giving them much of their resonance and savor. I've spent thousands of hours in the garden since that afternoon, and there is perhaps some sense in which all this time has been spent trying to recover the watermelon and the flush of pride that attended its discovery."

Such flushes of pride do not come easily. Pollan began his adult gardening life under the influence of Thoreau's ideology. Insecticides, the slaughter of mammals, and fences to cordon off the garden from wild nature were not part of his philosophy—that is, until he received from nature itself a bit of nasty comeuppance that made him think again. Thoreau might "grow [his beans] for woodchucks partly," but after listing the backbreaking tasks—turning the soil, toting heavy bags of manure and peat moss from the car, mixing these nutrients into the freshly prepared ground, then carefully sowing lettuce, broccoli, and cabbage seedlings in neat rows—Pollan had other sentiments. "Do all that, kill an afternoon, and see how you feel the next morning when this orderly parade ground of seedlings has been mowed down by a woodchuck out snacking," he challenges the reader.

In his war against the wily woodchuck, Pollan is a born loser. After discovering the animal's burrow and blocking its entrance with rocks, he finds to his chagrin that "the very next day the hole had yawned open and spit out the rocks and the soil. No doubt hungry from the work of excavation, the woodchuck had emerged from his burrow to sample a fresh planting of lettuce seedlings." Pollan now feels forced to at least consider the idea of fencing. However, he still opts to side with Thoreau. His perennial border is one in which "the aristocratic refinements of delphinium, baby's breath, campanula, and lady's mantle gradually give way to day lilies, a sloppy drift of evening primrose, an ill-mannered six-foot-tall clump of rudbeckia and, finally, to proletarian purple loosestrife, a weedy plant that grows around here." The point of this, of course, is to *not* have a fence interrupting the flow of the garden as it gradually merges with nature—an echo here of the aesthetic William Robinson propounded in *The Wild Garden*. And because he is an *American* gardener, Emersonian transcendentalism is there to reinforce this aesthetic choice: "We may no longer spell it out, but most of us still believe the landscape is somehow sacred, and to meddle with it sacrilegious." Virtuously, he concludes, "A fence could only wreck this garden."

But on second thought, so could woodchucks—not to speak of deer and invasive grasses. With chagrin, he reports, "My early efforts at harmonious design were lost on the surrounding landscape, whose inhabitants promptly sought to take advantage of my naïve romanticism." In a macho turnaround, Pollan takes "a Vietnam approach," with escalating measures to exterminate his marmot marauder, until the final one backfires—literally—when he ignites a gallon of gasoline poured into the woodchuck's burrow. This last murderous maneuver in his attack on the woodchuck ends as he watches "a black-orange fountain of flame flare out from the earth and reach for the overhanging olive bush."

It is at this point that Pollan realizes that the enemy is not the woodchuck but nature. A walk in the woods takes him to the ruins of Dudleytown, an abandoned nineteenth-century village with house foundations and former fields and gardens all reclaimed by weeds and forest. Like all ruins, they speak of nature's relentless reclamation of desolate places, and this brings out the Thoreau in him once more as he realizes that the garden is "a kind ecological vacuum that nature will not abide for long." There is a hierarchy to be destroyed here. Such is nature's way. Garden plants, rich in carbohydrates, fat, and protein, are at the top of the menu for woodchucks, deer, and raccoons, "flora's great levelers." Redistributing the nutritional wealth of the landscape, just as Thoreau encouraged after he gave up growing beans, they might be called nature's democrats, along with the weeds, insects, and other unwelcome garden guests. These include:

> First the cutworms, who saw off seedlings at ground level. Then the aphids, specks of pale green that cluster on the undersides of leaves, sucking the vital fluids from young plants until they turn a last-gasp yellow. Next come the loathsome slugs: naked bullets of flesh—evicted snails—that hide from the light of day, emerging at sunset to cruise the garden along their own avenues of slime. The cabbage loopers are the paratroopers of the vegetable patch: their eggs are dropped on the cole crops by troop transports disguised as innocuous white butterflies. Last to arrive is the vast and far-flung beetle family—Colorado potato beetles, Japanese beetles, Mexican bean beetles—who mount a massive airborne invasion beginning in midsummer.

So now Pollan must face the challenge of holding nature at bay without resorting to toxic chemicals. He must determine how, when, and with which agents in the gardener's arsenal of pest controls he should wage battle. Inevitably, this leads him back to his first solution. He admits that he is at last ready to put up a fence. Arsenic-treated, galvanized steel mesh no longer appears to be an abomination when the woodchuck merely paces its perimeter, and a solar-panel-powered, electric wire above it is going to give a powerful message to the voracious deer.

But a fence only takes care of the mammals. Insects don't respect fences, and as a post-*Silent Spring* gardener, Pollan is still loath to use malathion and other potent chemical pesticides. The answer is to not underestimate the intelligence of predators. For instance, "The ladybug is not smart, but she knows one thing exceedingly well: how to catch forty or fifty aphids every day without hurting anybody else." In the same spirit as Celia Thaxter importing toads to Appledore Island to take care of her scourge of slugs, he gets mail-order ladybugs from a company that sells "biological controls." The ladybugs can be kept in a refrigerator and spooned out onto infested plant leaves as needed. He tells us that from the same source you can obtain praying mantis egg cases. Sew these onto a tree branch, and after the weather warms up in the spring and the nymphs emerge, you will be amazed at the reflexes of this patient, seemingly motionless predator when it snatches flying insects right out of the air. A friendly bacterium, the milky spore, can infect a grub, which is the larva of the Japanese beetle and a favorite morsel for the mole. Dust the ground with these spores and you will halt the emergence of the Japanese beetle from its larval stage. This will prevent a hoard of beetles from chewing the leaves of your rosebush into lace, while at the same time, the grub-deprived moles will have to go elsewhere and cease tunneling under your lawn.

The moral of all this biological second-guessing? Pollan says:

> I won't know for a while whether I've completely solved my pest problem. But, puttering in my newly fenced garden, watching the mantises standing sentry on the tops of my to-matoes and the ladybugs running search-and-destroy missions among the eggplants, I'm starting to feel a lot more relaxed about it. . . . I still have much to learn, and there are going to be setbacks, I'm sure; gardening is not a once-and-for-all thing. Yet I think I've drawn a workable border between me and the

forest . . . [that] doesn't depend on technical invincibility. Nor does it depend on the benignity of nature. It depends on me acting like a sane and civilized human, which is to say, as a creature whose nature it is to remake his surroundings, and whose culture can guide him on questions of aesthetics and ethics. What I am making here is a middle ground between nature and culture, a place that is at once of nature and un-apologetically set against it; what I'm making is a garden.

Allen Lacy

A professor of philosophy and humanities, Allen Lacy (b. 1935) is also a prolific garden writer and editor. His books, which include *Home Ground: A Gardener's Miscellany* (1984); *Farther Afield: A Gardener's Excursions* (1986); *The Gardener's Eye and Other Essays* (1992); *Gardening with Groundcovers and Vines* (1993); and *The Inviting Garden: Gardening for the Senses, Mind, and Spirit* (1998); are compilations of short pieces he has written for *The New York Times* and slightly longer essays that have been published in *Horticulture Magazine* and other periodicals. As mentioned above, he performed an act of editorial midwifery in bringing Elizabeth Lawrence's *Gardening for Love: The Market Bulletins* to publication.

As is the case with other garden journalists, you can look at the table of contents or thumb through a Lacy book, picking out the titles that strike your fancy. And many do. However randomly you choose to read him, you soon discover that Lacy has a distinctive style and literary voice. In this he resembles other writers whose words grow out of their own gardens and whose thoughts come across as genial conversations so seemingly spontaneous that we sometimes feel surprised at the writer's depth of horticultural expertise and breadth of general knowledge. Also evident in Lacy's prose is a philosophical bent, and he is frequently apt to read into the garden metaphorical meaning.

Let us look at a snowdrop—no, scrutinize it—with him in *The Gardener's Eye*. You would think that because we are viewing it through an Eschenbach 10 Leutchlupe that we are studying it from a scientific perspective, but this is only partly the case. It is the flower's complex and subtle beauty that we are made to observe as Lacy describes the intricacy of its botanical structure:

> There turn out to be six flower segments, not just the three we see from on high. The outer petals are pristine white near the base, then banded with a contrasting shade of fresh lime green, then edged again with a thin band of white. On closer look, the band of green is not a solid band at all: it is composed of very narrow vertical green stripes, separated by even more narrow stripes of white. But green and white do not say everything about a snowdrop blossom. All six petals, inner and outer, surround a disk of overlapping honey-colored stamens, which in turn surrounds a white pistil.

Doesn't this sound a bit like Rousseau instructing Madame Delessert on how to excite the curiosity and develop the observational powers of her "little Botanist"?

But in addition to wearing the colors of Rousseau the botanist, Lacy also wears the colors of Rousseau the Romantic philosopher, the seeker of divinity in nature:

If gods make flowers, as ancient peoples believed, then the tulip was made by a tyro, the snowdrop by a god who had mastered the craft, a god with no need to resort to look-at-me colors like crimson and scarlet. "God," someone said, "is in the details." Having looked deeply into a snowdrop blossom, I know better what that means.

Lacy's vein of Romanticism is essentially an American one, for it is tinged with a religiosity that goes beyond Rousseau's rapturous reveries amid scenes of nature. Yet it is not quite the same thing as the pantheistic Transcendentalism of Emerson, which finds exaltation in nature's panoramic panoply. As we have just seen, Lacy's interest lies more with the plant than with the garden as such. His lovely garden pictures are not the same as those of Jekyll, vegetal vignettes within an overall garden composition; they are instead more intimate and spiritual celebrations of the revelations apprehended through the eye of the gardener. Indeed, "Closely Watched Plants," the title of one section of *The Gardener's Eye*, seems to sum up Lacy's approach.

As with Thaxter, when writing about flowers his eye is the eye of love. It is a caressing eye, and this is the source of his descriptive powers as a writer. Similes as well as metaphors abound in his prose, and here he is able to draw on his knowledge of biblical and classical literature. For example, "the pale green buds [of the chickweed blossom], smooth to the more distant eye, are as hairy as Esau," and "hollyhock seeds look like coal-black fossils of ammonites, the extinct mollusks whose name is itself a metaphor taken from the ram's horns associated with the Roman cult of Ammon." It is doubtful whether to-day's undergraduates will recollect the story of Jacob and Esau from the book of Genesis, and those of us who haven't sat in on Professor Lacy's humanities lectures are probably at a loss when it comes to differentiating the various Roman cults. But never mind. There are other more homey comparisons:

> The seeds of calendulas look like little caterpillars rolled into balls. . . . Oleander seeds resemble sea cucumbers, the seeds of scabiosa bring to mind the shuttlecocks used in badminton, and the comparison between bachelor's-button seeds and old-fashioned shaving brushes is irresistible. . . . Catnip seeds are the heads of little black monkeys, with two white eyes open wide with curiosity.

Drawing on the lore he finds in a rare book on certain evergreens, he goes into the multiple associations of the somber-hued yew:

> The ancient Egyptians regarded it as a symbol of mourning. The Greeks and Romans used its wood for funeral pyres; in Virgil's *Aeneid*, Dido immolated herself on a bed of yew. The Druids venerated the yew, and when England was Christianized, the yew became the graveyard tree of choice, continuing the pagan tradition. Medieval English plant lore held that yews fed on corpses and that after sunset the trees gave off poisonous vapors. . . .William the Conqueror's soldiers fought and won the Battle of Hastings with bows of yew. . . . George Washington is alleged to have proposed to Martha Custis beneath a yew. . .

What are we to think about the yew after this excursion into mythology and history?

For a plant so associated with the inevitability of death and with the exercise of military power, the yew is uncommonly docile. It is the poodle of the tree world, offering virtually no resistance to our desire to refashion it to our intent, to clip it and trim it to realize some pattern we have in mind. . . . Those with a taste for topiary can turn yews into dour green elephants and other shapes they would not assume of their own accord. I have, however, already announced my own preference, and it's a minority opinion. If there must be a yew in a garden, let there be but one, grown freestanding and unclipped, allowed in its own good time (as it may last for hundreds of years after I'm gone) to become the tree it is its nature to be.

This excerpt could fit nicely under "Y" in Perényi's alphabetical ordering of similarly quirky and freely opinionated garden essays. But Lacy also entertains the kind of green thoughts that can be compared to Deitz's. The section in *The Gardener's Eye* called "People and Places" consists of profiles and travel observations enlivened with relaxed erudition and interesting design description. He is, of course, familiar with the pantheon of garden writers who form the subject of this book and can speak of Thomas Jefferson, Gertrude Jekyll, William Robinson, Celia Thaxter, Louise Beebe Wilder, Vita Sackville-West, Charles Dudley Warner, Katharine S. White, and most especially Elizabeth Lawrence as he would of family friends. We are glad to watch them rise from his pages to receive appreciative appraisals.

Sometimes Lacy invites us to take a trip with him. On one such expedition, we arrive at Middleton Place, the historic plantation on the Ashley River a few miles north of Charleston, a few weeks after their show-stopping camellia and azalea displays. However, absence of flowers is not too much of a disappointment for one with a gardener's eye, especially since there was so much else to catch it.

> The crape myrtles had not yet begun, but the roses were in full bloom. The green of the grassy terraces where peacocks paraded, the deep blue of the Butterfly Oaks, the dark waters of Rice Mill Pond where swans glided by—these all bespoke a sense of place and of almost palpable time in Middleton's long history.

Looted in the Civil War and devastated by earthquake and hurricane, Middleton Place's beautiful gardens are punctuated with the ruins of earlier structures. But on the evening of his visit, a concert took place, and not surprisingly it brought out the philosopher in Lacy:

> The orchestra platform was right in front of the rubble of the old house, which had been damaged beyond repair by war and destroyed by earthquake. The concert opened with "The Star Spangled Banner." In the dawn's early light, the anthem's words proclaim, a patriot took pride. Our flag was still there. Both places and people can be survivors, and the comfort in that thought brings a lump to the throat.

In these often crepuscular days of national uncertainty it is good to have Lacy reminding us of such resilience in the face of adversity.

Conclusion

*I*n its original sense the word "amateur" connotes love, and the writers we have considered in this book are parties in a love affair between nature and the human imagination. They are amateurs as well in that, even when they have scaled the topmost branches of the tree of horticultural knowledge, they appear to approach gardening as a passionate avocation rather than as a form of professional employment.

In her introduction to Louise Beebe Wilder's *The Fragrant Garden*, Helen Morgenthau Fox writes:

> Although most amateur gardeners begin tentatively and with gloves on it is pleasant to see how they slowly change until the love for growing plants and arranging them artistically takes complete possession of them and the whole world is colored over with the hue of their hobby. . . . The further one goes along the road the more branches and related subjects one finds opening off from it and one has no idea whither these little side paths are going to lead. One thing is certain, however, that the people one meets as one travels are delightful, remarkably generous and invariably genuine. Their eyes are bright, their faces bronzed, their hands are full of callouses, and their hearts are brimming over with the love for plants.

Even when separated by distances of time or space, garden writers are inherent friends. If we should seek an overarching theme here, it is that of collegial comradeship among a non-exclusive circle that includes you, the reader, whether or not you are a gardener.

Afterword

DÉZALLIER & HIS DESCENDENTS:

*Three Centuries of Garden Writers in the Collection of
the New York Society Library*

❧❧❧

*M*orning light fills the Marshall Room at the New York
Society Library. The room where scholars view rare books,
the ones that usually remain in Stack Z under the supervi-
sion of a rare-book librarian, is very quiet. The book on
the long oval table is the 1728 English edition of Dézallier
d'Argenville's *The Theory and Practice of Gardening*, translated
by John James. It is a treatise meant to instruct gardeners
in the landscape-design methods responsible for the splendor
of the Sun King's gardens at Versailles. Taking note that its
publication date was 61 years before the French Revolution,
the researcher begins to turn the pages.

❧❧❧

Dézallier's *Theory and Practice of Gardening* is the earliest but not
the least of the treasures in the library's collection of books
on gardens and gardening. In terms of publication dates, its
holdings extend from this particular rare book to ones written in 2011. Though the collection is extensive, it is not comprehensive. It is possible that some early garden-related books,
including botanical dictionaries and horticultural calendars,
were destroyed or burnt during the Revolutionary War. It is

also suspected that British soldiers may have bartered some for grog. For these and other reasons, early ledgers housed in the archives list a number of books that are no longer in the collection. Nevertheless, many other books relating to gardens, botany, and horticulture appear in both the closed and open stacks within the building.

The Gardener's and Botanist's Dictionary (1797) by Philip Miller is a well-known classic. On the title page Miller describes himself as "gardener to the worshipful company of apothecaries at their botanic garden in Chelsea." There he grew exotic fruit such as the pawpaw (*Asimina*) and the pineapple (*Ananas*), as well as many other plants and trees. The library's two-volume edition, which weighs more than fifty pounds, contains thousands of entries.

At the end of the eighteenth century the advent of Romanticism altered the nature of garden literature. Although not in the canon of books about designed landscapes as naturalistic gardens, the library's 1796 edition of *Letters on the Elements of Botany* (1785) by Romanticism's apostle, Jean-Jacques Rousseau, is an important early title. Erasmus Darwin's *The Botanic Garden: A Poem in Two Parts* (1791) falls in the same category as an early introduction to botanical science. Like Professor Martyn's continuation of the pedagogy begun by Rousseau in his *Letters on the Elements of Botany*, it explains the system of botanical nomenclature developed by Carolus Linnaeus.

Also represented in the library's catalogue are some publishing landmarks in garden history from the first half of the nineteenth century. They include the writings of the

Scottish botanist J. C. Loudon and his wife Jane Loudon. In 1838 the former published *The Suburban Gardener, and Villa Companion,* followed two years later by *The Landscape Gardening and Landscape Architecture of the Late Humphry Repton, Esq.,* a new edition of this important treatise by "Capability" Brown's successor. Jane Loudon's pioneering handbook, *Gardening for Ladies* (1843) provided gentle encouragement and helpful advice for Victorian women gardeners. The library's battered and rebound copy is proof of its popularity.

Housed along with the Loudons' works in the closed stacks where books too fragile or valuable for circulation are kept is Sir Uvedale Price's three-volume *Essays on the Picturesque, as Compared with the Sublime and the Beautiful* (1810), an important exposition on landscape aesthetics. Other works of historic importance are *The Fruits and Fruit Trees of America* (1845) and *The Architecture of Country Houses* (1850) by the American horticulturist and landscape designer Andrew Jackson Downing. Also in the collection is Downing's *A Treatise on the Theory and Practice of Landscape Gardening* (1844). Once popular with newly affluent Americans eager to emulate English landscape practices on their Hudson River estates, it has now achieved rare-book status.

Time has not dulled the reputation of the great English garden designer Gertrude Jekyll. During her lifetime, in addition to her own garden at Munstead Wood, she designed many others in association with the architect Sir Edwin Lutyens. At the same time she managed to write some twelve books promoting her particular garden-design and planting style, an outgrowth of the Arts and Crafts movement in England. *Wood and Garden* (1899), *Roses for English Gardens* (1902), and *Colour in the Flower Garden* (1908) are among the many Jekyll books to be found in the library.

Like Jekyll, the Irish gardener William Robinson scorned contemporary Victorian gardening methods, including the use of carpet bedding, topiary, and elaborate waterworks. *The English Flower Garden* (1883), his best-known work after *The Wild Garden* (1870), was purchased by the New York Society Library in 1936. Fittingly, the library also owns a copy of *The Formal Garden in England* (1892) by the architect Reginald Blomfield, Robinson's literary opponent. The illustrations in Blomfield's book of lead vases, sundials, and terraced gardens are a world apart from the engravings of naturalistic garden scenes—casually composed flower borders and meadows with spring bulbs merging into woodlands—found in Robinson's books.

In the early 1900s the vogue for the Italianate style inspired a number of books on Renaissance villa gardens. Foremost among those in the library's collection is Edith Wharton's *Italian Villas and Their Gardens* (1904), with illustrations by Maxfield Parrish. The library also owns the 1951 edition of *An Essay on the Making of Gardens* (1909) by Sir George Sitwell. A meditation on the beauty of the old villa gardens in and around Rome, it has been described by the landscape historian John Dixon Hunt as "garden writing of the finest order and vision." The library's holdings also include *A Garden in Venice* (1903) by Sir Frederic Eden, a description of his garden on the Giudecca. As an aside, it is worth mentioning that Wharton's niece, the distinguished early twentieth-century landscape designer Beatrix Farrand, was a shareholder of the library, as was her grandfather, George Frederic Jones, and her father, Frederic Rhinelander Jones.

Celia Thaxter's *An Island Garden* (1895), with color illustrations by the American artist Childe Hassam, is another notable title in the library's catalogue. Thaxter's descriptions of her garden on Appledore Island off the New Hampshire coast are as evocative as Hassam's illustrations. Elizabeth von Arnim's *Elizabeth and Her German Garden* (1898) is also full of easy charm. The library's edition dates from 1900.

Moving into the early twentieth century, Maurice Maeterlinck's *Old Fashioned Flowers* (1905), with illustrations by Charles Falls, is another delightful book to take from the shelf. Originally published in 1907, the library's 1913 edition of *My Rock-Garden* by the alpine plant collector Reginald Farrer describes the rare flora this obsessive plant hunter brought back from expeditions to China, Burma, and other exotic lands, which he then planted in his Yorkshire garden.

Some mid-twentieth century treasures in the library include the books of Beverley Nichols, among which are *Down the Garden Path* (1932), *Green Grows the City* (1939), and *Garden Open Today* (1963). In addition, it possesses the charming classic *We Made a Garden* (1956) by Margery Fish and the 1983 edition of Russell Page's *The Education of a Gardener*, originally published in 1962. Vita Sackville-West is amply represented on the library's shelves. Her gardens at Sissinghurst Castle in Kent, the restored Elizabethan manor where she lived and gardened with her husband Harold Nicolson, served as the primary inspiration for her weekly columns in the *London Observer*, which were later published in a series of books. The library owns three: *In Your Garden Again* (1953), *More for Your Garden* (1955), and *Even More for Your Garden* (1958). Katharine S. White's *Onward and Upward in the Garden* (1979), a collection of her essays that first appeared in *The New Yorker*, is a paragon of good garden writing—instructive and amusing at the same time. Coming closer to the present day, there are illustrated volumes on gardening by Rosemary Verey and Penelope Hobhouse, which are informative from a horticultural point of view as well as beautiful to look at.

In addition, garden authors Francis H. Cabot, Lynden B. Miller, and Elizabeth Barlow Rogers are all longtime members of the library. Their books have special significance for this institution not only for this reason but also because of their literary excellence.

Cabot, a shareholder of the library since 1968, is a former chairman of the New York Botanical Garden and an expert plantsman. He is best known for the creation of two gardens: Stonecrop in Cold Spring, New York, and Les Quatre Vents in Charlevoix County, Quebec. *The Greater Perfection: The Story of the Gardens at Les Quatre Vents* (2001) has been described as "one of the best books ever written about the making of a garden by its creator."

Miller, who joined the library in 1970, is a public garden designer and the director of the Conservatory Garden in Central Park, which she restored under the auspices of the Central Park Conservancy in 1982. In *Parks, Plants and People*

(2009) she addresses the issues involved in public-space gardening. Miller also wrote the introduction to the 1990 reprint of Louise Beebe Wilder's *Colour in My Garden* (1918), one of six books by Wilder that are owned by the library.

Rogers, noted landscape historian and principal founder of the Central Park Conservancy, has researched several of her books at the library. These include *The Forests and Wetlands of New York City* (1971), *Frederick Law Olmsted's New York* (1972), *Landscape Design: A Cultural and Architectural History* (2001), and *Romantic Gardens: Nature, Art, and Landscape Design* (2010). The head librarian and members of his staff are understandably pleased that she is the author of the current volume, which discusses at greater length many of the works mentioned above.

❧❧

Late afternoon approaches. The table in the Marshall Room is piled with books. The researcher pauses, taking one last look at Dézallier d'Argenville's *The Theory and Practice of Gardening*. It is only the first of the literary gems in the collection of gardening books that the New York Society Library has acquired over the course of its more than 250-year history.

Harriet Shapiro
HEAD OF EXHIBITIONS
THE NEW YORK SOCIETY LIBRARY

Selected Bibliography

Arkell, Reginald. *Green Fingers: A Present For a Good Gardener*. New York: Dodd, Mead, 1936.

————. *Old Herbaceous*. New York: Harcourt, Brace, 1951.

Blomfield, Reginald. *The Formal Garden in England*. London: Macmillan, 1892.

Bowles, E. A. *My Garden in Autumn and Winter*. London: T. C. & E. C. Jack, 1915.

————. *My Garden in Spring*. London: T. C. & E. C. Jack, 1914.

————. *My Garden in Summer*. London: T. C. & E. C. Jack, 1914.

Cabot, Francis H. *The Greater Perfection: The Story of the Gardens at Les Quatre Vents*. New York: Norton, 2001.

Čapek, Karel. *The Gardener's Year*. Translated by Geoffrey Newsome. Brinkworth, Wiltshire: Claridge Press, 2003.

Darwin, Erasmus. *The Botanic Garden: A Poem in Two Parts*. London: J. Johnson, 1791.

Dash, Robert. *Notes from Madoo: Making a Garden in the Hamptons*. New York: Houghton Mifflin, 2000.

Deitz, Paula. *Of Gardens*. Philadelphia: University of Pennsylvania Press, 2010.

————, ed. *The Bulletins of Reef Point Gardens*. Bar Harbor: Island Foundation, 1997.

Dézallier d'Argenville, A. J. *The Theory and Practice of Gardening*. London: Bernard Lintot, 1728.

Downing, Andrew Jackson. *The Architecture of Country Houses*. New York: Appleton, 1850.

————. *The Fruits and Fruit Trees of America.* New York: Wiley and Putnam, 1845.

————. *Rural Essays.* New York: George P. Putnam, 1853.

————. *A Treatise on the Theory and Practice of Landscape Gardening.* New York: Wiley and Putnam, 1844.

Durand, Herbert. *My Wild Flower Garden: The Story of a New Departure in Floriculture.* New York: G. P. Putnam's Sons, 1927.

————. *Wild Flowers and Ferns: In Their Homes and in Our Gardens,* rev. ed. New York: G. P. Putnam's Sons, 1925.

Earle, Alice Morse. *Old Time Gardens, Newly Set Forth.* New York: Macmillan, 1901.

Eck, Joe, and Wayne Winterrowd. *Our Life in Gardens.* New York: Farrar, Straus, Giroux, 2009.

————. *A Year at North Hill: Four Seasons in a Vermont Garden.* Boston: Little, Brown, 1995.

Eden, Frederic. *A Garden in Venice.* London: Country Life, 1903.

Elizabeth [Elizabeth von Arnim]. *Elizabeth and Her German Garden.* London: Macmillan, 1898.

Farrer, Reginald. *In A Yorkshire Garden.* London: Edward Arnold, 1909.

————. *My Rock-Garden.* London: Edward Arnold, 1907.

Fish, Margery. *We Made a Garden.* London: Collingridge, 1956.

Hobhouse, Penelope. *The Country Gardener.* Oxford: Phaidon, 1976.

Jefferson, Thomas. *Thomas Jefferson's Garden Book 1766–1824.* Edited by Edwin Morris Betts. Philadelphia: American Philosophical Society, 1944.

Jekyll, Gertrude. *Children and Gardens.* London: Country Life, 1908.

————. *Colour in the Flower Garden.* London: Country Life, 1908.

————. *Roses for English Gardens.* New York: Charles Scribner's Sons, 1902.

————. *Wall and Water Gardens*. London: Country Life, 1901.

————. *Wood and Garden: Notes and Thoughts, Practical and Critical, of a Working Amateur*. London: Longmans, Green, 1899.

Johnson, Hugh. *Hugh Johnson in the Garden: The Best Garden Diary of Our Time*. London: Mitchell Beazley, 2009.

Lacy, Allen, ed. *The American Gardener: A Sampler*. New York: Farrar, Straus, Giroux, 1988.

————. *Farther Afield: A Gardener's Excursions*. New York: Farrar, Straus, Giroux, 1986.

————. *The Gardener's Eye and Other Essays*. New York: Atlantic Monthly Press, 1992.

Lawrence, Elizabeth. *Becoming Elizabeth Lawrence: Discovered Letters of a Southern Gardener*. Edited by Emily Herring Wilson. Winston-Salem: John F. Blair, 2010.

————. *Gardening for Love: The Market Bulletins*. Edited by Allen Lacy. Durham: Duke University Press, 1987.

————. *The Little Bulbs: A Tale of Two Gardens*. New York: Criterion Books, 1957.

————. *Lob's Wood*. Cincinnati: Cincinnati Nature Center, 1971.

————. *Through the Garden Gate*. Chapel Hill: University of North Carolina Press, 1990.

Loudon, John Claudius. *The Landscape Gardening and Landscape Architecture of the Late Humphry Repton, Esq.* London: Longman, 1840.

————. *The Suburban Gardener, and Villa Companion*. London: Longman, Orme, Brown, Green, and Longmans, 1838.

Loudon, Mrs. [Jane]. *Gardening for Ladies; and, Companion to the Flower-Garden*, 1st American ed. Edited by A. J. Downing. New York: Wiley and Putnam, 1843.

————. *The Ladies' Flower-Garden*. 5 vols. London: William S. Orr, [c. 1855–59].

————. *My Own Garden; or, The Young Gardener's Year Book*. London: Kerby & Son, 1855.

Maeterlinck, Maurice. *Old Fashioned Flowers and Other Out-of-door Studies*. New York: Dodd, Mead, 1905.

Miller, Lynden. *Parks, Plants, and People*. New York: Norton, 2009.

Miller, Philip. *The Gardener's and Botanist's Dictionary*. London: F. C. & J. Rivington, 1797.

Nichols, Beverley. *Down the Garden Path*. Garden City, NY: Doubleday, Doran, 1932.

————. *Garden Open Tomorrow*. New York: Dodd, Mead, 1968.

————. *Green Grows the City*. New York: Harcourt, Brace, 1939.

Page, Russell. *The Education of a Gardener*. New York: Random House, 1983.

Paul, William. *The Hand-Book of Villa Gardening*. London: Piper, Stephenson, and Spence, 1855.

Perényi, Eleanor. *Green Thoughts: A Writer in the Garden*. New York: Random House, 1981.

Pollan, Michael. *Second Nature: A Gardener's Education*. New York: Atlantic Monthly Press, 1991.

Price, Uvedale. *Essays on the Picturesque, as Compared with the Sublime and the Beautiful*. 3 vols. London: J. Mawman, 1810.

Robinson, William. *The English Flower Garden*. London: J. Murray, 1883.

————. *Gravetye Manor, or Twenty Years' Work Round an Old Manor House*. London: John Murray, 1911.

————. *The Wild Garden*. London: John Murray, 1870.

Rogers, Elizabeth Barlow. *The Forests and Wetlands of New York City*. Boston: Little, Brown, 1971.

————. *Frederick Law Olmsted's New York*. New York: Praeger, in association with the Whitney Museum of American Art, 1972.

———. *Landscape Design: A Cultural and Architectural History*. New York: Harry N. Abrams, 2001.

———. *Romantic Gardens: Nature, Art, and Landscape Design*. New York: Morgan Library & Museum; Boston: in association with David R. Godine, Publisher; New York: Foundation for Landscape Studies, 2010.

Rousseau, Jean-Jacques. *Letters on the Elements of Botany: Addressed to a Lady*. Translated by Thomas Martyn. London: B. and J. White, 1796.

Sackville-West, Vita. *Even More for Your Garden*. London: Michael Joseph, 1958.

———. *In Your Garden*. London: Michael Joseph, 1951.

———. *In Your Garden Again*. London: Michael Joseph, 1953.

———. *More for Your Garden*. London: Michael Joseph, 1955.

Sitwell, George, Sir. *An Essay on the Making of Gardens*. London: John Murray, 1909.

Strong, Roy. *Garden Party*. London: Frances Lincoln Limited, 2000.

Thaxter, Celia. *An Island Garden*. Boston: Houghton Mifflin, 1895.

Thoreau, Henry David. *Walden*. Boston: Ticknor & Fields, 1854.

Verey, Rosemary. *A Countrywoman's Notes*. London: Gryffon, 1989.

———. *Rosemary Verey's English Country Gardens*. New York: Henry Holt, 1996.

———. *Rosemary Verey's Making of a Garden*. London: Frances Lincoln, 1995.

Warner, Charles Dudley. *My Summer in a Garden*. Boston: Houghton, 1870.

Wharton, Edith. *Italian Villas and Their Gardens*. New York: Century, 1904.

White, Katharine S. *Onward and Upward in the Garden*. New York: Farrar, Straus, Giroux, 1979.

White, Katharine S., and Elizabeth Lawrence. *Two Gardeners: Katharine S. White and Elizabeth Lawrence; A Friendship in Letters*. Edited by Emily Herring Wilson. Boston: Beacon Press, 2002.

Wilder, Louise Beebe. *Colour in My Garden*. Garden City, NY: Doubleday, Page, 1918.

———. *The Fragrant Path: A Book about Sweet Scented Flowers and Leaves*. New York: Macmillan, 1932.

———. *My Garden*. Garden City, NY: Doubleday, Page, 1916.

Wilson, Emily Herring. *No One Gardens Alone: A Life of Elizabeth Lawrence*. Boston: Beacon Press, 2004.

Wolseley [Frances Garnet], Viscountess. *Gardens: Their Form and Design*. London: Edward Arnold, 1919.

———. *In a College Garden*. London: John Murray, 1916.

Yang, Linda. *The City Gardener's Handbook: The Definitive Guide to Small-Space Gardening*. North Adams, MA: Storey, 2002.

ILLUSTRATION CREDITS

Frontispiece, Pages 11, 13, 15, 18, 22, 27, 30, 46, 49, 50, 56, 66, 67, 71, 79, 82, 90, 91, 95, 100, 108, 120, 123, 124, 127, 131, 143, 173. Collection of Elizabeth Barlow Rogers.

Pages 38, 42, 44. Collection of The New York Society Library.

Page 21. Courtesy of Judith B. Tankard.

Pages 136, 137, 230, 234. Photographs by Elizabeth Barlow Rogers.

Pages 150, 154, 155. Photographs by Joe Eck.

Page 179. Photograph courtesy of Wing Haven Gardens, Charlotte, North Carolina.

Page 194. Pen and watercolor drawing by Simon Dorrell. Courtesy of *Hortus* quarterly.

Page 223. Photograph by Steven Wooster. Courtesy of Little, Brown and Company.

Pages 246, 247. Photographs by Sara Cedar Miller. Courtesy of Central Park Conservancy.

Set in Van Dijck,
Garamond, and Caslon types.
Printed by Four Color Offset.
Designed by Jerry Kelly.